Evacuees

Evacuees

GROWING UP IN
WARTIME BRITAIN

GEOFFREY LEE WILLIAMS

AMBERLEY

The Williams family *c*. 1934.

This edition first published 2013

Amberley Publishing
The Hill, Stroud
Gloucestershire, GL5 4EP

www.amberleybooks.com

British Library Cataloguing in Publication Data.
A catalogue record for this book is available from the British Library.

ISBN 978-1-4456-1334-5 (print)
ISBN 978-1-4456-1346-8 (ebook)

Typesetting and Origination by Amberley Publishing.
Printed in the UK.

Contents

For my grandchildren,
Sofia, Alexander, and Joseph

Prologue and Acknowledgements

By weaving the events of the Second World War with its impact on his boyhood, Geoffrey Lee Williams develops a unique and amusing book which seeks to question the widely held view that during the Second World War British children played no real or recognised part in the war, except as evacuees who as a result might have suffered traumatic psychological damage or physical deprivation. The vast majority of evacuees arguably benefitted from their unexpected wartime experiences to a greater or lesser extent according to their age, class and location.

This vivid account is a personal history of the Second World War as perceived and experienced by the Williams twins from south-east London, who were nine at the outset of the war and precocious teenagers by its close. They both wished nothing more than to be allowed to take part in the war itself and they actually achieved this in their own way: hubris and fate made it an unforgettable experience.

The Williams twins, in a simplistic way, appeared to understand the true nature of the unfolding conflict which the Munich Conference of September 1938 made almost inevitable. They acquired the alarming mindset which became an obsession: that the waging of this conflict was for them more important than their education and schooling. They were simply unaware of the official view that British children were not, and could not, play a direct part in the waging of war.

Of course, historically, the twins were correct: children had always fought in wars throughout European history as they did in the Hundred Years' War and the Thirty Years' War. Both boys perhaps glibly dismissed the view that by the mid-twentieth century civilians, including women and children, should be classed as non-combatants according to utopian conventions and interpretations of international law. They simply took the view that total war included everyone. They were blithely ignorant of the view that in more civilised days the distinction between combatants and non-combatants expressed the deep moral conviction of mankind arising from the Christian tradition of the just war. In the Western world at least there was the belief that international war must be fought according to certain humanitarian rules.

At the early age of nine Geoffrey and Alan Lee Williams decided what they were going to do for the duration of the war, or for what little time remained of their lives. They instantly knew that this war was not simply a re-run of the First World War, but a war of necessity involving the survival of their way of life. Yet for the most part they enjoyed the excitement and danger rather more than the fear of destruction and death. The story unfolds and reveals the unique opportunities which war itself made possible in a boyhood like no other. This book, therefore is a memoir based on a narrative about wartime childhood. It is written by the elder of the two brothers.

I wish to acknowledge the assistance of my son, Jeremy, for typing the initial draft of this book and, with my twin brother Alan, for reading and making suggestions and corrections.

Last but not least I must acknowledge the encouragement and patience of my wife, Janice. Her readiness to read, edit, and amend all the drafts of the manuscript was a formidable task given that it was written by me in longhand.

Introduction

In the autumn of 1939 my twin brother and I faced
having to leave home for the first time. Within days of the
declaration of war against Nazi Germany on 3 September
1939 we were, like countless thousands, evacuated to the
towns and the countryside beyond London in the first of
our four evacuations between 1939 and 1944.

Yet between these relatively short evacuations, we were
back in London and, during the final phase of the German
attacks on southern England in 1944/45, we were able, at
long last, to play our part in the war effort when we both
enrolled in the National Fire Service [NFS] as fourteen-year-
old messengers. We wore the uniforms with pride. However,
in reality, our modest part in the war begins much earlier
when we were young children, just on the threshold of pre-
teen maturity. In fact, even before 1939, during the period
of appeasement that stretched from roughly 1936 to 1938,
we sensed the growing threat to our settled existence. We
were at war before the war actually started. Obviously, we
could have known nothing about military strategy, but we
almost instinctively grasped in a simplistic way the true
nature of the unfolding conflict.

Later we were to learn about modern war in relation
to aerial bombardment from the conceptual thoughts of
the great theorists like Billy Mitchell, Seversky, Douhet

Geoffrey & Alan – the Promenade, Margate, *c.* 1938.

and Lord Trenchard. Yet even at the age of six we sensed in a paranormal way that the bombing of cities was to be a crucial part of modern war which could lead – and did – to much material damage and loss of life. We, as young schoolboys, began almost subconsciously to prepare ourselves for the psychological experience of the impending war arising from ruptured friendships and the reality of fear and death. In a curious way being identical twins heightened our shared belief that we would die in this war, which the Munich Conference of September 1938 almost made inevitable.

We picked up the vibes of war during Neville Chamberlain's desperate bid to avoid conflict with Hitler's Germany. In 1938 we were on our annual summer holiday in Clacton, rather than our usual resort Margate, for what turned out to be the last such holiday for ten years. There we solemnly developed a premonition that we would shortly either be injured or worse in a dreadful war. This erroneous prediction does much, subsequently, to explain our extraordinary conduct between 1939 and 1945 which so shocked our parents and dismayed our friends.

We acquired the alarming mindset, which became an obsession: the waging and winning of this war was for us more important, much more important, than our schooling or the official dogma that children could not directly take part in or contribute to the waging of war. Civilian casualties which, by definition, included the women and children of Britain and of course those of Nazi Germany were palpably drawn into the conflict. In an act of policy during the final phase of Total War in Nazi Germany, teenage *Hitler-Jugend* soldiers actually fought against the Allied advance.

Although our generation of British children, living in a democracy, are perceived as having played no official part in the war, this memoir contradicts that belief.

The Second World War, *pace* Angus Calder, was a people's war: only the senile, the infirm, the sick or the mentally ill were silent or oblivious to the constant stress that this titanic conflict involved. The first half of the twentieth century reached its climax with the utter defeat of Germany, and ultimately Japan, by which time we were on the threshold of manhood.

Alan and I, right from the start and in a rather inchoate way, knew instinctively rather than intellectually that this would be a classic war of attrition. The bits and pieces of the debris of war fell everywhere and anywhere irrespective of gender, class, age or nationality.

This is our story, as seen through the eyes of growing children. We grew up rapidly in the most dire of circumstances, the long-term effects of which lasted a generation. The memories of childhood can be recaptured with surprising clarity by the supreme effort of recollection and empathy. However, context matters and, as in the war memoirs of adults whose accounts have proliferated over the last seventy years, both of us, now in our eightieth year, have come to certain well-considered conclusions about the past. Of course the past is never quite dead but it does cast light on the present.

We are today privileged to live in a debellicized society, a pluralist democratic post-modern state whose citizens now face a very different threat. The new threat is no less real with ordinary civilians overwhelmingly the victims. But this is not new; 48 per cent of casualties in the Second World War were civilians.

After the war Alan went on to a parliamentary and political career and I eventually went into university teaching for over forty years.

We both believe that our separate identities and shared beliefs constitute a sound basis for this joint interpretation of a wartime boyhood, which many others of a similar age could readily match and mimic. Our identities were initially developed in the limited circumference of time and space which constitutes this book.

We both stress that our shared memories need not be false or illusory: we are the product of our memories which can distort the past as much as it can validate it. Of course none of us can remember all the minutiae of childhood experiences, as many of our activities are now beyond recall since most of them are of a routine and inconsequential nature. But as people now live longer, our capacity to remember some of our earliest impressions of life during the period of the Second World War could have merit and be of value to future generations.

Few of us can really remember much of what happened to us before the age of five. After that our ability to recall events is well established as scientific research shows that our brain cells get better and faster. Medical experts say that we reach full absorption capacity at nineteen where we retain two hundred bits of information per second, exceeding that of the fastest computers. Yet after the age of twenty-seven there is decline and a falling away of our brain cells which die off at a rate of ten thousand a day! Clearly now in our eightieth year – we were born in November 1930 – some form of deterioration is likely, but, as Saint Augustine averred when he was asked whether he was ready for celibacy, 'Well, not just yet.' The truth is that we were more or less fully grown by the age of ten in a cultural and strategic environment which left no real room for childhood. We therefore entered our teenage angst in our mid-twenties with all of the consequences that flow from prolonged immaturity when most of our peer group were adults. Does this explain why we are still working? No retirement for us! This book is therefore written in part to warn against growing up too soon. Beware of what you desire.

Finally this book does have, to some extent, a wider and deeper significance than just a narrative about our evacuation and wartime experiences. It amounts to more than the sum of its parts because our joint rejection of formal education for the duration of the war can be seen as a metaphor for our scepticism about conventional attitudes towards the conduct of the war. Even though we barely understood what was involved in total war, still less how best to fight it, we realised intuitively what the war was about. Nazi ideology was obsessed with basic problems of economic and social organisation. The aims of the National Socialist Party were so fundamental as to justify the term revolutionary. The Hitlerzeit wished to change the nature of German society, and by extension that of Britain had it been defeated and occupied, and were so sweeping that it stands comparison with that of Jacobinism in 1792 or Bolshevism in 1917. Hitler possessed an ideology that was by definition incompatible with the preservation of peace in Europe. The ultimate aim was the eradication of reason and tolerance which were the joint pillars of a democratic and pluralist society. Although I cannot claim that we saw things as clearly as this, or that we were well informed about political ideology in a sophisticated manner, we saw it was a war between right and wrong. The defence of political democracy was a public good, a view widely shared by the British people between 1939 and 1945.

We boys, rightly or wrongly, gave the waging of war our absolute commitment from a position of physical weakness and intellectual immaturity, in relation to which our actual contribution to the outcome of the war itself was negligible. Yet we made a persistent attempt to go to war nonetheless. The reader must decide whether we were myopic or just plain, straightforward duffers.

Geoffrey Lee Williams
Cambridge, 2010

1

The Great Disruption

The day war broke out we were elated. At 11.15 a.m. on 3 September 1939, the entire family sat facing our small radio to hear the Prime Minister speak to the nation. We had never heard his voice before, although we were all familiar with the BBC announcer Alvar Lidell who frequently read the news with impeccable clarity and authority. He solemnly introduced the Prime Minister who was sitting in the Cabinet Room of 10 Downing Street. His address to the nation included these words, which Alan and I, over a number of months, committed to memory – throughout the war we were able to mimic to perfection:

> This morning, the British Ambassador in Berlin handed the German government a final note stating that unless we heard from them by 11 o'clock that they were prepared at once to withdraw their troops from Poland, a state of war would exist between us. I have to tell you now that no such undertaking has been received and that consequently this country is at war with Germany.

We all fell silent. Mother looked dismayed, Dad looked depressed and our sister Gwen was in a state of shock. We twins were elated. This was the war we had expected and in our wide-eyed innocence, was the big event that we knew would transform all our lives. We were at war and this would surely lead to the closure of all the schools and our school days would be over. Needless to say we turned out to be totally mistaken. Worse was to follow; we were to be evacuated to the countryside away from the expected bombing and this meant the equivalent of a boarding school in the middle of nowhere.

The preparations for war were now pretty obvious and even before war was declared on 3 September 1939 plans were in place to put up air-raid shelters in public places. Households such as ours were provided with an 'Anderson' shelter. One of these was erected in our garden and was to be shared with our closest neighbours, the Phillips family. For a long time it remained unused and was badly flooded during the wet winter of 1939, since it was not really ready for use and was in fact largely neglected except as an extra space for storage.

We boys found it highly suitable for war games and deployed our tin and lead toy soldiers on its roof that was conveniently covered in sand and earth, thus providing good imitation battlefield conditions. We defeated the German Army several times a day since the realities of real war had not yet impinged on us. There was actually little concern about the war to begin with and the slowness of events contributed to an early return home from our first evacuation to a small village near Ashford in Kent.

Yet it all started so differently. 3 September was an exciting day for us boys, overshadowed only by the thought of evacuation to some remote place. Then suddenly, after the Prime Minister's broadcast to the nation announcing that we were now at war with Nazi Germany, the air-raid siren sounded. We all ran for cover. This was a false alarm, one which became a regular occurrence.

Despite all the fuss we noticed that few pet dogs had, as instructed by the government, been put down and that the cat population continued to grow. The exception was our pet dog, taken by our father to an early grave at the Kidbrooke Blue Cross

Kennels. The blackout came with predictable consequences. We boys were given torches that were never to be shone into the sky during an air raid although, to begin with, the bombers failed to materialise. Instead two very pretty Army nurses arrived to lodge in our house and sleep in what had been our bedroom, so naturally we were expected to sleep somewhere else. But where in such a small house? This soon became starkly clear; this war was going to prove to be a massive disruption of our lives and we would be expected to leave home very shortly.

The bombing had yet to start and rationing was slowly introduced as food supplies dwindled and shipping losses increased. The real heartbreak came when we had to leave 22 Mayday Gardens, perhaps never to return. Our war had started and we boys did our best to exploit our comparative advantage. This was where the BBC came into our calculations in a rather surprising way. During the successive political and constitutional crises of the mid-1930s we had listened as a family to the BBC. But we boys started to mimic the delivery and accent of Stuart Hibbert, the chief BBC News announcer, since we admired his solemn and authoritative delivery of the national news. His light baritone voice personified the best English delivery and accent without sounding too exaggerated. We simply imitated him. Later, when our voices broke, we adopted the baritone delivery of Bruce Belfridge, another BBC wartime announcer, who similarly personified the classical period of middle class dominance on British radio.

Within days of the declaration of war we were evacuated, or as we saw it exiled, to the small village of Hartley in Kent. We went with Paul Packman, a school friend, and were sent to the village school which was teeming with other evacuees from south-east London. This was a private evacuation arranged by Paul Packman's father who drove us to Hartley in his Ford 8 car. We were sad to leave but enjoyed our first experience of travelling in a car as it was possibly the only one, apart from a rather splendid open-top car owned by the father of our close friend Harry Savage, in Mayday Gardens. In fact Mr Savage rarely ever drove the car and once the war started it was hoisted up on bricks for the duration. Hartley was only thirty miles or so from where we lived in London. It was then a delightful village where we were billeted with a family, whose son John, aged nearly nine, was roughly our own age. John was to die tragically from electrocution while playing with his impressive electric railway set just a few years later.

Between 1936 and 1939, prior to our evacuation to Hartley, we had attended our local infant school, but by 1938 we had a premonition about the unfolding future. To begin with all seemed normal and Alan and I reflected on this as we adjusted to life at the local school in Kent. We were depressed, confused, and utterly at a loss as to how we could survive without our mother and father and we sank into contemplative despair offset by a conscious attempt to understand and relive the past. We attributed a highly coloured and romantic mystique to our home in Blackheath, but we were both too young to have proper understanding of the past, or to grasp the present, and the future looked bleak.

Between us we charted how we had got to where we were and to a lesser extent where we stood in relation to the war. Our childish and superficial impression of the past began to assume a significance and clarity that, as far as we could judge, very few boys of our age seemed to possess. We took stock of who we were and tried to imagine or recollect what it meant to us to have a permanent home. Thus getting back home became an obsession.

At the age of five we had moved into 22 Mayday Gardens on the Normanhurst Park Estate in Kidbrooke, Blackheath – Mayday was the SOS for danger. This account is, therefore, about our visions and dreams of childhood in crisis. To us 22 Mayday Gardens was more than just a nice house; it was what this war was about. We deduced that in thinking about it we gave to the war effort its moral and ethical justification, which went beyond the deep personal loss and longing for our parents. Life as we saw it centred on our home.

This semi-detached house cost £695; it was freehold and was purchased on a mortgage with the Halifax Building Society. Repayments were, to begin with, on a weekly basis of 17s and 4d, but later my father paid by monthly cheque. The house itself, built by New Ideal Homesteads, had a spacious hall, a front room, a dining room and a kitchen on the ground floor with three bedrooms and a bathroom on the top floor. The garden could be entered from French windows in the dining room, as well as through the kitchen door, and was of a decent size with two small apple trees surrounded by various fruit bushes. At the bottom of the garden my father grew vegetables. There was a tall fence at the bottom of the garden which gave us privacy, but on both sides we could see our neighbours and they could see us through a see-through fence some 5 feet high.

We were a family of five consisting of Alan and myself, identical twins, our sister Gwen who was some nine years older,

John, Geoffrey, Paul and Alan – Hartley, Kent 1939.

and our parents. Alan and I took to our new house with relief since we had escaped from the cramped and dank conditions of a basement flat in Deptford. In our new house everything seemed so bright and new. We now had hot water available to us and two lovely open fireplaces in the front room and in the dining room. The kitchen was neat and modern with enough room for a breakfast table, a gas cooker, and a small pantry and faced out to the garden which had a cottage ambience.

The house was well positioned near green fields and vast wooded areas so, for us, it was a semi-paradise. Within a one mile radius was Woolwich Common and the splendid military academy built by James Wyatt. Our father, Alfred, had served in the First World War as a medical orderly, having joined the Royal Army Medical Corps underage in his mid-teens. He married my mother, Alice, in 1920 having proposed marriage to this strikingly beautiful woman in the teeth of her mother's opposition; our grandmother on the maternal side was fiercely against her daughter marrying a Thames lighterman. She surely deserved someone better. Yet lightermen were the aristocracy of the Thames who frequently wore dark suits and bowler hats when acting in a supervisory role.

Alfred proved to be a good father and a faithful husband. His personal experiences in the First World War made him unwilling to discuss it; his shaking hands and partial deafness attesting to the physical, and possibly emotional, injury inflicted during the carnage of the Battle of the Somme. He had left school at the age of fourteen and, after working at Guy's Hospital as a medical assistant and later working for Dr Salter, the Labour MP for Bermondsey, he had volunteered to join the Army in 1915. He served for five years until his discharge in 1920. Before discharge he contracted the deadly flu virus which was to take so many lives but not, thankfully, his. The Army sent him for treatment to St John's College, Cambridge, where a wartime hospital unit had been established and where, two generations later, his grandson was an undergraduate. He was an intelligent and thoughtful man but he became, for a time, totally alienated by the conduct of the First World War and disillusioned with the British state. He joined the Communist Party but left when he discovered how devious and duplicitous they were in plotting a Leninist takeover of the State, the Trades Unions, and the Labour Party. Alfred Williams was no stooge as events were to show. He was a stout patriot at heart but somewhat cynical about flag-waving and resented inherited privilege.

It was with great pride that he took us to the ceremonial Church parades held in front of the Royal Artillery Barracks at Woolwich on most Sunday mornings. The troops marched by while the Royal Artillery band played regimental music applauded by a considerable crowd. We boys were particularly fascinated by the bronze Chinese guns that stood in front of the Royal Military Academy, where officers were trained for the Royal Artillery, Britain's oldest regiment. In some strange way we felt part of it all. A few years later the garrison church was hit by a V1 'doodlebug', destroying the historic church that had dominated the two tram routes to Beresford Square, Woolwich. Nearby stood the charming Royal Artillery Theatre which survived the bombing of the Second World War, then hosted the excellent Wheeler and Salisbury Repertory Company, before being knocked down in an unrivalled act of vandalism by the War Office.

We were privileged to live so close to so many historic places and, as a family, we paid isolated visits to London, from Trafalgar Square to the Regent's Park Zoological Gardens, and from Horse Guards Parade to Buckingham Place. Nearer to home was Greenwich Park with its splendid Royal Observatory and the meridian line that gave the park its global significance.

Most interesting of all, to us boys, was the statue of General Wolfe, which was next to the Royal Observatory standing at the highest point of Greenwich Park. General Wolfe was our favourite eighteenth-century British general because of his victorious expedition of 1759 against the French general, Montcalm. Wolfe and his army defeated the French by scaling the Heights of Abraham at Quebec, although both commanders were killed in the subsequent battle on the Plains of Abraham. Our personal knowledge of this war was already detailed for young boys of our age. General Wolfe caught our historical imagination and we rejoiced in his success. Our somewhat one-dimensional interest in war became our comfort zone since we were less adept at applying ourselves to formal schooling.

This British victory, now largely neglected, established *British* supremacy over Canada. Our boyhood interest in Canada was reinforced by the splendid uniforms worn by the Royal Canadian Mounted Police, attired in red tunics and wide-brimmed hats. Their red colour also matched the colour of London's buses and trams which made us think that London was truly the centre of the universe.

By 1939 we had a child-like impression of where we stood in relation to our family and neighbourhood, while attending our local infant school was a truly memorable but short lived experience. Henwick Road School was a solid building of conventional design as were most, if not all, of the London County Council schools in south-east London.

To get to school we had to walk through a council estate from where the numerous children accounted for the ever growing number of pupils. Although we were only there for a few short years before the war, this experience played a large part in developing our collective social consciousness. We were puzzled as to why so few of our school friends came from where we lived on the Normanhurst Estate, which was itself growing fast. Indeed, during the first three months of 1934 alone sales here totalled 1,284 houses with an average of 223 sold each week. This part of England was thriving in the wake of the great recession and London's growing prosperity looked like an irresistible national trend.

The layout of our burgeoning estate was based on modern town planning principles; the roads were wide with green verges on either side, curved to avoid any monotony of appearance, and the houses were so situated as to give character to the environment. They appeared to be good solid houses sold at low prices. Indeed, life in Mayday Gardens took on an air of permanence and settled activity. But this was not to last with the coming of war that we boys so foolishly welcomed as the excitement of war overwhelmed our poorly developed sensibilities. Little did we know it, but we were about to undergo a painful and unforgettable experience as was our entire generation.

Geoffrey – Henwick Road School *c.* 1938.

2

A Suburban Dream

On our return home from Hartley, life, somewhat deceptively, returned to normal. This was the period of the 'phoney' war, the prelude to the real thing. We, and our neighbours, were adapting to the idea of a long war. Who were our neighbours and who were we? We were soon to discover the answer to both those questions. In our childish way we little understood the true nature of the unfolding drama as war impinged itself on our minds. As Alan and I later recalled, our neighbours had considerable awareness of the growing political, strategic, and constitutional crises in the run-up to the war itself. We ourselves could not express our feelings since our linguistic skills and our vocabulary were yet to grow. In fact we invented a language of our own, as twins tend to do, called 'gummage'. But our individual and joint recollections of an age and of a generation now in the limbo of history are curiously vivid and real. Clearly going to school in 1936 was for us, as for most children, a real turning point; it took us out of our own cocooned 'twin' world and away from the restrictions of our over protective parents. My mother especially provided us with an environment more suited to a royal or an aristocratic existence. We were therefore quick to see both Princess Elizabeth and her sister, Princess Margaret Rose, as soulmates. Later in life, for just fifteen minutes, I was to become Princess Margaret's unlikely dancing partner and, although I

Alan, Aunt Rose and cousin Betty, and Geoffrey and his mother – Herne Bay
c. 1936.

certainly lacked her ballroom dancing abilities, she seemed
both elegant and attractive in a surprisingly seductive way.

As boys we both liked and owed much to the influence
of women and girls. This has remained a constant part of
our experience, if a somewhat troubled one, having had
five wives between us! However, both of us have eventually
enjoyed over thirty years of married life in our middle age.
My mother Alice was a beautiful woman and devoted mother
and was a loyal wife to my father who could be irascible
and domineering. None of my mother's sisters liked him,
but all three of them, plus one brother, recognised him to
be a man of integrity and honesty who was devoted to his
wife and family.

Our relationship to our brilliant sister Gwendoline was
more interesting. We adored her just this side of idolatry.
She was some nine years older than us and nine times more
intelligent. She was also very attractive, thus greatly admired
by the opposite sex whom she disdainfully ignored as she
piled up her academic lead over them. She went up to Oxford
in 1944 just as Alan and I were expelled from school for the

last time and were about to enter the workforce without a single academic qualification to our names. Nevertheless, we were precocious and ahead of our contemporaries in our grasp of societal trends and political realities. Our native cunning enabled us to conceptualise and understand events with considerable verve and insight which, while it compelled attention from our school masters, evoked total disbelief given our nonchalance towards formal learning and attainment. It took several decades, after leaving school in 1944, for us to recognise our errors and lack of common sense. All that mattered to us was the war and its outcome. We were excited by, and enjoyed, the war more than most people at the time realised.

The trouble really started at school well in advance of the war. We clearly suffered from an attention deficiency, arising perhaps from our relationship as identical twins that produced a satisfying environment of imagination and action far beyond realms of reality. When we began to allow the real world to impinge the excitement of it nearly overwhelmed us as great events unfolded. We wished to be a part of the action and everything else was subordinate to it.

Events unfolded with some rapidity between 1936 and the outbreak of war in 1939. Some of these events were political and constitutional as well as strategic in character. We were, as odd as it may seem, aware, or partially aware, of their importance. The aftermath of the slump and its dire consequences washed over us to some extent leaving a residue of consciousness about real life in Britain and beyond. Our hostile response to the growth of German power in Europe and our growing interest in the abdication crisis of 1936 astonished parents and friends but meant a lot to us, and our close relations were puzzled by our interest in events well beyond our years. We were developing a sense of what was happening to us, and to Britain, which belied our age and experience. We displayed a strong desire to be noticed and admired, as do most children, but being identical twins we attracted a great deal of attention.

This attention-seeking behaviour inspired Alan to join an attractive nine-year-old violinist, Jean Stoddart, in the school concert. She needed a pianist to accompany her for a difficult piece by Mozart and Alan volunteered to join her in her moment of glory at three days' notice. He neither read music nor could play the piano, although my mother could, so Alan asked her to teach him to read music and to play the piano in time for the concert on Monday. I was astonished by his temerity and optimism and his failure and personal humiliation was inevitable. It was a puzzle as to why he ever thought he could learn such skills in so short a time and so, rather than lose face, he went to school on the Monday with his arm in a sling to cover his inability to play the piano. Rather than risk being exposed as a reckless illusionist, Alan had temporally got Jean Stoddart's respect, as well as the school's acceptance that his wrist injury alone explained why he could not play the piano as promised. To Alan talent and image were important attributes of his personality and character.

Yet it was amazing that anyone believed Alan's excuse, still less believed that he could play the piano to a standard to match the brilliance of the young blonde he admired so much. Actually, she never realised her true talent whereas, ironically, Alan did, as a politician and parliamentarian, where his deceptive arts were more appreciated. He hated being underestimated: this to some extent could also be said of Britain.

Britain between the wars was a complex and fast-changing society and our schooling itself reflected the sectarianism and class jealousies which we both sensed existed on a small scale in our school's circumscribed catchment area.

The school covered an area consisting of lower-middle- and working-class children. Mayday Gardens, where we lived up to and periodically during the war, was really a lower-middle-class neighbourhood. It comprised a mixture of white-collar workers and skilled or semi-skilled blue-collar workers, all of whom shared in common a mortgage on freehold houses of varying sizes and shapes and who felt themselves to be the new social order.

Alan and I walked to school firstly through open green fields then through the large council estate that gradually enveloped the area around Henwick Road School, then an infant school, but which, post-1944, became a large elementary modern school for both boys and girls.

As war approached our lack of interest in schoolwork, apart from reading, raised the anxiety of our parents. We were now regarded as educationally backward and were compelled to undertake a series of tests which once completed seemed to show that our eyesight was normal but that our vocabulary was possibly retarded because of our use of 'gummage' – our special language. This self-invented vocabulary with its impenetrable syntax was incomprehensible to those, including our parents, who were anxious to discover what we were saying to each other and why we seemed so strangely isolated in our own little world. The reality was that we could relate to the real world if, and when, we chose but on balance preferred not to do so – with good reason! The outside world was not a nice place but, of course, our knowledge of it was limited and one-dimensional. We liked anything political and the idea of war, in a general sense, took up most of our curiosity and interest, and peace was just the interval between one war and another. Germany took the same view as Hitler always denied that Germany was defeated in 1918. We boys always claimed that Britain had won the First World War with a little help from our allies, but we also saw how that war had weakened British power.

The legacy of the First World War loomed large in our childhood, although this was rarely referred to in ordinary conversation at home. Dad never discussed it openly, but clearly his duties left him shell-shocked and partially deaf. His hands periodically shook when he came under pressure and his inability or unwillingness to discuss the horrors he had endured at such an early age made him impatient and short-tempered. Yet he never allowed his experience of the war to overcome his sense of proportion in living a good life. We boys were encouraged to read the newspapers he bought, either the *Daily Herald* or the *News Chronicle,* as well as our own weekly diet of *The Children's Times*, and later, wartime comics, which continued to be published and which projected an image of the war itself well suited to young minds.

We listened to *Children's Hour* on the BBC and enjoyed Commander King Hall's weekly political commentary. We liked items about the British Empire which figured in red on large areas on the atlas and maps that we kept among a complete collection of Charles Dickens books bought by my father in a bid to increase our literacy. Actually we could read quite well, though our spelling was idiosyncratic, a trait that has remained, for Alan at least, a lifelong problem, though it is more amusing than serious, so he therefore prefers the spoken to the written word.

I, in particular, compiled a scrapbook on Germany and France but knew little about Britain's relations with them. Only Britain really mattered to me. Both of us were proud of the size of the Royal Navy as well as the size of the Empire. We rightly demonised Adolf Hitler and, although we could not speak German, we disliked his rasping delivery and thought him evil – hence our interest in the coming war.

The diplomatic front aroused much less interest but later we began to follow this very closely with the approach of war. Our schooling took a back seat to such an extent that an inevitable crisis point was reached and questions were raised as to whether we should be sent to a special school for backward children. This alarmed us both and, in the short term, motivated in us a renewed interest in formal schooling.

However, with the growing certainty of war and the intermingling of great events, this simply lapsed again into total disinterest. Our parents were drawn into some unpleasant theories about us. Dad, in particular, decided on one simple explanation; 'We were a couple of duffers.' Gwen, our sister, was much less convinced of our stupidity so she drew our attention to the *Concise Oxford Dictionary*'s definition of a duffer, which included a reference to 'inefficient, useless or stupid person'. This infuriated my mother and she and Dad fell out over Dad's caustic reference to her twins. 'They are not imbecilic,' she starkly asserted, 'but they do need help.' The educational experts provided little comfort and they diagnosed a deeper problem which carried some medical credibility. Alas, there might have been some truth in what they were saying about possible brain damage at birth, perhaps made worse by our addiction to the taste of lead paint which we licked off our bedroom window frames. We both became something of a medical mystery since, in all other respects, we were physically normal. No real conclusion could be reached, however today we might have been diagnosed as being somewhat autistic, to which a seminal 1970s study by Michael Stutter suggests twins are prone. Yet for autism to be diagnosed in a child they must exhibit social impairment, communication difficulties, and a variety of non-social problems. In general terms this means a child failing to comprehend other people's emotions, displaying repetitive behaviour, and having restricted interests. None of this really seemed to apply to either of us even if both of us did tend towards rigid routines combined with a preference for strict punctuality in our daily lives. In any event, before steps could be taken to sort out our educational difficulties much greater problems began to overshadow our lives.

I remember very clearly, as does Alan, a number of events which led us to emerge from the cocoon in which we had enveloped ourselves in the run-up to the war, and we can now identify several events which changed everything for us. Our lives would never be quite the same as our suburban home suddenly became much more vulnerable.

We had, as mentioned earlier, returned to London after our brief stay in Hartley and resumed school at Henwick Road early in 1940. The period of the 'Phoney war' was drawing to a close as winter passed into spring and the tedium of school beckoned. Something like a deceptive normality descended on the Williams' household. Most of our school friends were back. John Bray, the son of a senior warrant officer serving in the Royal Artillery as an instructor at the Royal Military Academy Woolwich, had never left home and was delighted to see us back. Harry Savage returned home to where his father was a technician in a local factory, and finally, Barry Earps, the son of a clerical officer now commissioned in the Home Guard. Later Peter Panterlow returned; he was a much older boy of considerable intelligence who suffered from bad eyesight arising from a birth defect and his return home completed our close circle of friends. Before the war, Peter's mother had been a musician in the famous Ivy Benson all-girl band. Slightly outside the group was Paul Packman, whose father was a foreman at Ford's Motor Company, but as Paul attended a different school, we only saw him from time to time. His father owned the only car, a Ford 8, still running after the petrol rationing brought private motoring to an end. Mr Packman had managed to overcome petrol rationing by sticking a gas tank on top of his car to our great amusement. This provided enough fuel for short journeys although we did notice that Mr Packman never walked anywhere.

Mayday Gardens now saw the slow departure of men of military age – including the call-up of the Walls Ice Cream delivery man! At the bottom of the road, on a sizeable sports ground, the RAF took up residence in the pavilion and, on the cricket square, the crew installed a barrage balloon. Alan and I soon befriended the RAF ground crew, who were later to be replaced by women. The Women's Auxiliary Air Force personnel, most of whom were strikingly feminine, were very quick at getting the balloons' erected once German aircraft approached. The girls became our temporary fixation in the absence of Jean Stoddard who was evacuated in 1939 and was never, alas, to return to Henwick Road School. We thought that the war would never begin properly and that the only excitement was the fuss created by the ARP Warden's attempt to impose the blackout. Our family struggled to black out everything completely but, as the days lengthened, the need to do so diminished somewhat. By then the blackout was, none the less, well in place, in fact so much so that going to Cubs at the local Scout hut required us to take a torch for both illumination and safety. Attending Cubs was the real highlight of the week but we wanted to do more. Our attempt to join the Air Raid Precautions [ARP] was met with contempt by the wardens, who told us to wait another five years before applying. We were utterly determined to be of use so we started to collect waste paper as part of the national drive to recycle paper. We collected tons of newsprint on a scale that led our Cub mistress to recommend us for the Scouts National Service badge. She, in the meantime, promoted us to 'sixers' and we duly received the badge on the eve of the Battle of Britain. During the Blitz we also collected loads of shrapnel which was widely scattered over the roads after the Ack-Ack guns had fired, often in vain, at approaching German aircraft.

The fall of France was the first great event which led to our total immersion in the war and the total loss of our peacetime existence. Like everyone else around us we saw the evacuation of the British Expeditionary Force from Dunkirk as a heroic defeat as well as the prelude to the real war. Our interest now centred on how and why France was defeated. We knew nothing about the fighting beyond what we heard on the BBC. For us, and for our friends of the same age, the true significance of the loss of France was essentially secondary to the blackout, food rationing, the carrying of gas masks, and the need to produce identity cards on demand to the police. These were the really pressing matters of the day. We listened to the BBC for news of the war, at 9 a.m., 1 p.m., 6 p.m. and 9 p.m. and for the latest developments concerning a possible German invasion of Britain, which we feared was certain to follow the defeat of France and the Low Countries. The fear of invasion was palpable as we waited for it to begin.

Alan and I looked at maps and compiled diagrams of the likely places where German paratroopers could land. The presumed existence of the 'Fifth Column' disfigured our excitable minds as spring and summer unfolded. We were convinced that Nazi spies were everywhere and we had to do something about this before it was too late. We kept a sharp eye on our neighbours' house, at the bottom of our garden. They had already been prosecuted for blackout offences which was never a trivial matter. As self-declared pacifists they had refused to recognise that we were at war. In our eyes this assumed sinister and malign intent on their part as later, during the Blitz in the autumn, they deliberately left their lights on throughout the house. Once the air-raid warning had sounded local people screamed abuse at them for their deliberate recklessness. Yet nothing was done until, during one night attack, we enlisted our taciturn Scottish neighbour armed with his .303 Home Guard standard issue rifle to shoot out the windows of the fully-lit house. We regarded this incident with pride as during the course of future German attacks the house at the bottom of the garden was fully blacked out. The occupants were foolish and misguided but they were not, as we surmised, actual German agents. They were in fact Quakers, not Nazis, and one was crippled and the other nearly blind. Yet in the blackness of the night in nearby Castle Wood a man, presumably deliberately, flashed his torch at low-flying German bombers in a systematic attempt to attract their attention. Who was he? And what was he trying to do? We had spotted the flashing light coming from deep in the woods as we made our way home from Cubs one evening just as a German reconnaissance plane, possibly a fighter, swept in to locate possible targets. We were determined to catch the man with the torch since the police, the ARP, and our parents failed to conduct a real search of the woods. As far as the authorities were concerned this was just another example of public hysteria about possible fifth columnists in their midst. Actually the feeling that German sympathisers and agents were active in the area grew slowly into a conviction shared by many. Certainly Alan and I were convinced that something was afoot. We formed a small group of Cubs into a unit armed with sticks and staves in order to carry out an extensive search of the wood, which we searched during daylight hours mostly on Saturday mornings. Jack Wood had existed for centuries and was covered with ancient trees and, during the height of the Blitz, it became an unwelcome depository of unexploded bombs. We frequently found suspicious holes which, in a few cases, contained unexploded incendiary devices, but were in fact mostly the homes of the local fox population. Apart from loads of shrapnel we could find no trace of the German agent. We did eventually discover a lair, an encampment of twigs, grass and branches, built to provide some protection for a tiny number of people. We decided to put it under close observation and only left the wood when serious battles raged overhead as Spitfires and Hurricanes sought their German quarry.

Then one afternoon our painstaking efforts were rewarded in a most unexpected way and in a manner that we little understood until our early teens. Two semi-naked people covered by an army greatcoat, a man and a woman, were rolling on top of each other in a most extraordinary fashion involving intensive activity, accompanied by screams of pleasure rather than appeals for help. Twelve of us watched this activity in the knowledge that it was something lovers did in private rather than in public. Love and war had become intertwined and so the search for the German agent was abandoned for the time being.

The school holidays had started and with them the dog fights above the fields and woods of southern England. This conflict was more interesting than the trysts of lovers though we (ourselves) later found sex to be the most exquisite form of human excitement – but not just yet! Our obsession with possible Nazi agents gave way to the belief that they lived amongst us rather than running around in the open after dark shining a torch.

The real war for us came with the start of the London Blitz, as disruption was followed by actual destruction. Death became commonplace and damage widespread. Our suburban home was not immune as Mayday Gardens itself came under direct attack. The war was now awfully close. The continuous night attacks were now more frequent than the daylight raids. The ARP wardens added to our anxiety with their hysterical response to the faintest glimpse of light. Our local warden frightened Mum half to death with his piercing scream of 'put that light out'.

3

The Blitz and Evacuation Again

Great events now impinged on our daily life. Many of our father's friends had taken their Thames tugs to the beaches of Dunkirk to help in the rescue and the Battle of Britain had become for us a crucial moment in British history. As young boys we gathered as much knowledge as we could about former British national victories and defeats which we retold to our hastily formed unit of Cubs preparing to intercept invaders. The horrors of Passchendaele and the Somme were played out with our toy soldiers on top of the Anderson shelter before the assembled group of Cubs/spy hunters of between eight and ten boys. Excitement followed excitement as news vendors started to pick up on Britain's love of sporting competitions by chalking up such headlines as, 'Biggest Raid Ever – 78/26 England Still Batting!' This sporting metaphor in particular raised our morale and reinforced our growing sense of pride in the RAF as the conflict in the air took its course.

This life-and-death aerial combat was relayed daily by the BBC commentators as a feature in the news reports throughout the summer of 1940. We listened to the BBC in rapt attention, in contrast to our school work which had now come to a complete halt. But, to our dismay, the holidays were soon over and we prepared ourselves for school with a mixture of impending boredom and disdain.

Fate, however, combined with our own hubris, intervened with a cataclysmic series of events on the afternoon of 7 September 1940.

The sun shone all day long and this glorious weather had prompted us to organise a game of cricket on the flat grassy land at Little Wood nearby. We had just finished play at around 4 p.m. in time for tea with the expectation of drawing stumps that evening when the German airforce had other ideas and, before we could resume, the air-raid siren sounded. What we were about to witness was a raid of such size and consequence that we were convinced, as was the entire nation, that the German invasion was about to begin.

Daylight raids against the capital, which began on that fateful day, followed a series of isolated night raids on the capital during the last half of August. We knew that some of these bombs had fallen nearby on the Old Kent Road and we had also heard that the RAF fighter station at Biggin Hill had been attacked on 30 August. Twenty-nine RAF men and eleven civilians had been killed and many injured in an accurate, low-level, bomb attack that was never admitted to by the authorities at the time – we were told about it by the RAF crew at the bottom of the road who were manning the barrage balloon. 7 September was, for us, the first really momentous day of the war, when 350 bombers raided the East London dock area. They came with a strong fighter force that was itself attacked by our own fighters, mostly Spitfires, as far as we could judge, and we personally counted over seven hundred aircraft in the sky at the height of the engagement. According to our neighbours, Mr & Mrs Phillips, who originally came from Bermondsey, the Surrey docks had gone up in flames possibly killing many of their relations who worked there.

The bombing then continued without a break for seventy-seven nights. Our school, though undamaged, was closed but our joy was short lived as the prospect of another evacuation loomed to our great dismay. We learned later that the air battles in the week between 7 September and 15 September were decisive in turning the tide of battle. The entire family felt elated that the Germans had suffered great losses at the hands of the RAF. Yet our disappointment in having to abandon our cricket match on that fateful Saturday was replaced by a growing fear of invasion to follow.

This was no time to leave London and we begged our parents to stay to defend Mayday Gardens, now threatened as never before. Though it is difficult to get into the mindset of ten-year-old boys, we felt that we simply had to stay at home. Dad had other ideas. The London docks had had to close temporarily and he had accepted a job in Scotland as a munitions inspector at a small arms factory, so the entire family was to move there as quickly as possible. The good news was that the evacuation to Scotland would be for no more than six months. Dad was expected to return to London sometime in the spring of 1941 when the London docks, it was hoped, would be in full swing. We boys regarded the abandonment of our home as a massive defeat.

The move to Scotland was not without drama. A heavy raid on the city of Coventry on 14 November actually delayed our departure, though we were unaware of this. Dad later told us that the whole of Coventry had been destroyed. Whereas us Londoners could always move to other parts of the great city, where shops and services were still operating, the enormous damage to a relatively small town like Coventry had shown how deadly the Germans could be in launching these concentrated attacks. Mum and Dad were obviously trying to persuade us to leave London as soon as possible.

It was evident from even censored reports that the immediate situation in Coventry was as desperate as that experienced during the first weekend attack on the East End of London. According to John Bray, our local military expert and friend, the British Army had been sent into Coventry to help restore order and clear up the bomb damage. John Bray's father, who was always well informed on these matters, said that Birmingham, Southampton, Manchester, Sheffield, Portsmouth, and Leicester had been badly bombed and the raids were continuing. The Williams household discussed how best to get to Scotland as soon as possible and how to secure the house in our absence. Both of our parents discussed the matter with neighbours, all of whom were now pessimistic about the outcome of the war. Alan and I tried to remain cheerful and our mother, Alice, had the last word by saying that going to Scotland was the only thing we could do in the circumstances. Gwen, our greatly admired sister was still away from home, living in South Devon, where her school had been evacuated in 1939. Gwen had sent a bitter letter in which she had said she expected the Germans to arrive in Devon in a matter of days; should she come home now? Dad wrote back immediately to say that she should stay where she was and that we were off to Scotland and would be in touch as soon as possible. Gwen wrote an alarming reply saying that Britain couldn't rely on either Russia or America in time to save us. Dad replied optimistically that America would not allow Britain to fall and that they would intervene soon but, according to Peter Pantelow's father, we would be compelled to sue for peace within weeks. The mood of defeatism was all-pervasive and made worse when Dad left for Scotland alone with the rest of the family due to follow him shortly afterwards.

Mayday Gardens was in disarray. One night, from our bedroom window, we spotted a Heinkel 111 directly overhead caught in the white glare of a searchlight. It started to weave violently and, at full throttle, dived in attacking mode into the searchlight beam before suddenly disappearing into the dark void of the night. We fled to the safety of our Anderson shelter dressed in our pyjamas. We were terrified. Was this the end for all of us?

Life in London for my mother had become intolerable so she willingly packed our bags and prepared for our departure and the three of us were on our way to catch the over-night *Flying Scotsman* out of King's Cross. Our journey to the station was very difficult indeed, since wartime travel was made very dangerous by the constant air raids. We caught a bus travelling along the Old Kent Road, since it was thought that a bus was more likely to get to its destination than a tram, which was more likely to be delayed by damage to the track or indeed the overhead wires and cables. The local train services were badly disrupted, so we had taken the right decision. As the bus inched its way towards King's Cross, bombs appeared to be falling all around us and yet they always seemed to fall beyond our vision. The noise though was overwhelming. The helpful and cheerful bus conductor advised us to travel on the lower deck near to the back of the bus where he stood and where the passengers got on and off. He whistled the popular song, 'Roll out the barrel' and in between his musical performance made clear announcements about where the next stop was. His reassuring commentary was at odds with the fate of the bus directly in front of us, which had just been hit by the blast of a bomb that also destroyed a couple of shops and a bus shelter located about 75 yards ahead of us. Our bus swerved past at speed and continued its intrepid journey. When we finally arrived at King's Cross our jolly and brave conductor told us that we should not worry about catching the *Flying Scotsman* because it was always escorted by a Spitfire. Once in the station we were surrounded by Scottish soldiers noisily boarding the train in large numbers. We managed to find an empty second-class carriage and were joined by two other passengers plus an army major. A friendly Scottish woman told my mother that the Royal Family had left London and were now living somewhere just outside Edinburgh. The train departed forty minutes late in growing darkness and without the Spitfire escort as far as we could see. Outside our carriage in the dimly lit corridor soldiers were standing and sitting in large numbers. They were mostly small and vigorous Glaswegians who pestered Mum and tried to flirt with her throughout the journey. Mum simply ignored them for she knew that any encouragement on her part would possibly result in them behaving in an over-friendly fashion.

In the meantime, Dad was waiting at Waverley station in Edinburgh to take us to a local hotel. On the train we were surrounded by the soldiers who drank increasing quantities of whisky and beer purchased at every stop the train made. The army major sitting opposite Mum ordered the soldiers to stop pestering her and he summoned a sergeant to ensure that they did so. At long last we arrived and we all went to a hotel in Princes Street in the gloom of the early morning. We stayed in one room and shared a large bed only too thankful to be together again. We were exhausted and we soon fell into a deep sleep to be awakened by the familiar sound of an air-raid siren, but the 'all clear' was given a few minutes later.

The next day, after a late breakfast, we made our way by local train to Roslyn, which was about ten miles from Edinburgh, arriving in mid-afternoon without any fixed lodgings and no certainty of a welcome. We need not have worried because the kindness we were about to experience completely eviscerated the misery of the journey.

In truth, though, Scotland was neither our easiest nor most enjoyable experience. We integrated into the local school without too much stress and soon joined in the morning break-time habit of eating a hot mutton pie sold each day by the local butcher to the hungry lads of the village. The school lessons were perfunctory and the teaching uninspired and dull. The best teachers had obviously been called up for war service. To us boys Scotland was a foreign place as we understood little of what they said in their thick accents, which came across as bellicose and rude. This was an entirely false impression because this early experience was soon belied by the generosity of the Scots when, having arrived from Edinburgh with our heavy suitcases, we initially had nowhere to stay. We needed to find temporary accommodation while looking for a more permanent place to stay for at least three to four months.

Dad's place of work was not far away so our parents thought we should live close to his factory and luckily, as we trudged along the road in the fading light, we spotted a large white farmhouse standing about one hundred yards from the factory. The house was substantial and surrounded by numerous outbuildings some of which were in a sad state of disrepair. Like the refugees we were, we approached the main door of the house in some disarray and Dad rang the front-door bell. After a long delay a middle-aged woman with white flowing hair appeared and explained that callers normally arrived at the back door. The front portion of the house was closed for the duration of the war. The farm, she said, was not being fully worked as the farmer was serving in the Army overseas. Dad explained our plight and said that he actually worked in the factory nearby and that his family had joined him to escape the heavy bombing of London. He said we were looking for lodgings of a more permanent character, but that right now we just needed overnight accommodation. The woman stared hard at us boys and suddenly said in an unfriendly way, 'No.' She could not offer accommodation to children since an elderly, retired teacher lived in a couple of rooms on the ground floor of the house and that 'Miss

White wanted to be left undisturbed'. Suddenly Miss White herself emerged. She possessed a kindly face and had that charming manner of the Edinburgh bourgeoisie. She smiled and said that in the circumstances she would not object to us staying the night but beyond that she felt that her health, which was not that good, would suffer if we stayed given the likelihood that the twin boys would be lively and boisterous. 'I know a lot about wee boys,' she said, for she spoke with great authority having spent her life teaching them. At least we had a bed for the night and the promise of a good Scottish breakfast to set us up for the hunt for accommodation the next day.

The best reassurance, however, that we could give Miss White was for us to behave impeccably and so we responded to our mother's plea to behave and be quiet. We spoke to her in a subdued way and called her 'Miss White' very politely. After breakfast Miss White agreed that we could stay in the vacant rooms on the ground floor if we behaved and respected her space. She felt that this was the least that she could do given our plight and the need to keep our family together. 'The Blitz in London,' she said, 'must have been terrifying for you. Hitler is a wicked man,' and so we actually stayed in this delightful house from November 1940 to the early spring of 1941 when we returned south.

Keeping out of Miss White's way was made much easier as we both caught whooping cough and were confined to our beds. Alan suffered more than I did and gave real grounds for concern. However, we were physically strong despite our somewhat premature birth. In fact we were so tiny at birth that it was in the London press when the *News of The World* reported our survival as a miracle. Later as young adults this was a newspaper we had no wish to appear in given its sensational treatment of miscreants but already we were national news!

Now approaching our tenth birthday at the end of November 1940 we had great stamina and a strong will to live thanks to the attention of our devoted mother. Scotland's bracing air and the comfort and warmth of a well built house capable of withstanding the exceptionally cold winter of 1940–1 further guaranteed our continued well being.

The war now seemed but a distant memory and the excitement of it had now given way to more normal concerns. We eventually made friends with a local boy whose father was an estate manager responsible for a considerable parcel of land where we could play and explore and so we played, often in deep snow, in the fields facing the Pentland Hills. But the sound of war was never far away as German air raids were made on Glasgow and Edinburgh. One day after the local siren sounded we were told by a couple of elderly ARP wardens to return to the safety of the farmhouse right away, though no air-raid shelter existed there. On another occasion when the air-raid siren sounded the wardens appeared from nowhere to urge us to take cover, 'Get a horse,' they exclaimed vehemently and so, thinking that they needed a horse, we led a rather aged nag, whose days were clearly numbered, over to them. 'No not a horse, get into the house.' Once again the local accents had confused us and made us look foolish.

Having recovered from whooping cough we resumed our schooling. One day towards the end of our stay, as we walked home high above the white foaming waters of the River Esk, just below the remains of an old castle, we were set upon by two older boys of about twelve or thirteen. They shouted abuse at us for being English and, although we had encountered them before, this time they seemed to mean business as, because of our premature birth, we were relatively small for our age and therefore appeared vulnerable. The attack started with a vicious kick up the backside followed by a savage blow to the face. Both of us had been used to the rough house of the playground but this was different. The bigger lad suddenly called off the attack and slowly walked away but the second, heavier boy had other ideas. He pushed us both down the bank beneath which the river flowed and, standing upright, preparing to deliver a final blow in a bid to push us into the deep water below. Little did he know about us! We had, in previous pushing and shoving incidents in the school playground, devised a defensive tactic where Alan, being a bit bigger and stronger than me, played the crucial role in our joint response. I moved quickly behind this youth and crouched down into a little ball. Meanwhile Alan pushed the attacker over me in a swift movement which sent him tumbling down the bank towards the water. He was last seen in the water close to the far bank of the river as we fled at top speed to the safety of the house on what was to be our final day in Scotland as, the next day, we all retreated south to London in better shape and humour than on our arrival in Scotland. We were ready to go home but the German air force was ready and waiting, although Alan and I feared the German bombers rather less than the two Scottish ruffians who so nearly knocked us both into the fast-flowing water of the River Esk.

Yet we all retained fond memories of Scotland. My own lasting impression was of a visit with Dad to the Glasgow Empire, the graveyard of English comedians. Alan was still recuperating from whooping cough and so missed a very Scottish pantomime. I never understood a word of what was said but found it exciting and funny – though possibly for all the wrong reasons. Yes Scotland was certainly distinctive and different. It was our haven for a short time, but our return to London seemed surprisingly encouraging since we quickly detected a change of national mood as the pessimism of late 1940 had given way to a stoic determination to carry on. Our own personal fortunes, however, were about to take a dramatic nosedive. There was little doubt that 1941 was to prove to be a bad year for us all. We therefore gave a prudent welcome to the New Year, at least we were back home, but things about were to change rapidly, and for the worse.

4

The Escape to Devon

1941 proved to be something of a turning point for us as well as for the nation. Before the year's end Britain would have acquired two powerful allies aligned against Nazi Germany. But in Mayday Gardens the year started in a disastrous manner that left our beloved house and our neighbours in a state of shock.

Our arrival home from Scotland started well with our return to school and some semblance of normality descending on us and our friends. The nightly bombings had almost ceased, even though daring daylight raids continued to wreak havoc on the economy and on energy supplies, both of which were essential to the waging of total war. Alan and I felt differently about the war now, as we had come to realise that we were wrong to be so enthusiastic about the war itself, which was perhaps the first sign of a growing anxiety on our part. We spent our spare time, since schooling had been reduced to just two hours a day, assembling an arsenal of pots, pans, and garden railings as our contribution to the building up of the strength of RAF bomber command. These items were to be melted down into the necessary sinews of war by turning them into tanks, guns and aircraft although, as we learned after the war, much of this material had remained unused and collecting this ironware contributed next to nothing to the war effort. In good faith we had helped in a small way with the removal of gates and wrought iron fences for the greater good of the war as, in those days, we all blithely accepted whatever the government proposed or thought was necessary to win the war. Winston Churchill's rhetoric stirred the nation into a passionate belief in the rightness of our cause and that cause was the defeat of Hitler's Germany by whatever means. Now, at the age of ten, the war was about to collide violently with our personal hopes and aspirations.

The land mine struck at about 9 p.m. on Wednesday, 19 March 1941, just as the nation tuned into the BBC's nightly news bulletin, although we were asleep in the Anderson shelter and totally unaware of either of the news or of the land mine slowly descending over the cemetery behind the houses across the road. It arrived stealthily, as our neighbours, as well as Mum and Dad, made their way into the house to boil a kettle to make a cup of tea that had become a nightly ritual once the bombing activity appeared to pause. That night carnage and destruction awaited us all; we were suddenly woken up in the shelter by a very loud explosion and a blinding flash which brought havoc and death to our beloved Mayday Gardens. Remarkably we were unhurt but our house was partially destroyed and, in all, nine people were killed and twenty-six injured that night, with thirty-seven houses completely destroyed in a very small road. The following day we spent the entire time clearing up the mess as well as seeking out our close friends, Harry Savage and John Bray, both of whom had survived and were in good spirits.

Harry's house had suffered less than ours, but John's house was now, essentially, a wreck. Our eardrums were stinging and singing for a week. Alan went really deaf for a day or two before his hearing returned, although he was left with earache. 22 Mayday Gardens had lost its roof, all its windows, and most of the downstairs furniture, including irreparable damage to Mum's upright piano, which was punctured by bits of glass and masonry. In our bedroom shards of glass made an unholy mess of our school uniforms and underclothing. Worse still there was a gaping hole where the roof had been and it soon started raining. Also there was no gas or electricity and the water supply was badly disrupted.

The real heroes of the night were Alfred Williams, our Dad, and Sergeant Tilburn of the Metropolitan Police, a near neighbour. After the explosion they both ran across the road to help the injured and the dying. Sergeant Tilburn used his huge height and strength to hold up the heavy debris enabling my father to burrow into small cavities to pull out some of the injured. This rescue operation was quickly supported by the rescue service and auxiliary fire service who, together with the ambulance crews, attended 'the incident' as such situations were formally described. We boys were sent back to the shelter together with Mum to get what sleep we could in what turned out to be a very long night. As we lay in our bunks recovering from the shock effect of the night's carnage, we had time to reflect. We knew that the damage done to our house would certainly take days, if not weeks, to repair, even though the outer structure, with the exception of the roof, had withstood the blast quite well. The damage done to our house would, therefore, almost certainly mean a third evacuation. It was clear to me that we would be sent to join our sister, Gwen, in South Devon once both suitable accommodation and a good school could be arranged, but neither proved easy to secure before we left to join Gwen.

Gwen played a decisive role in this process which took several weeks to accomplish. In the meantime, we adjusted ourselves to going to our local school each day for two hours. Lessons were frequently interrupted as we spent much of the time in the air-raid shelter because daylight raids continued in a sporadic way. Although we could not know this, Hitler, in the high summer of 1941, would turn against Russia, his nominal ally, although by that time we were living in the delightful seaside town of Teignmouth in Devon. Before we left the gas and electricity had been restored in our house and some of the windows replaced by cellophane imitation glass, although the middle part of Mayday Gardens was still a bomb site leaving a large area for us to play with our friends. We had lost several close friends and several playful dogs, but realised that an extraordinary number of cats we thought lost reappeared, although one just sat forlornly on the front doorstep of a non-existent house. Of course we knew from our neighbours, the Phillips, and indeed from Dad, that we had got off lightly compared to the dock areas of Deptford and Bermondsey, south of the Thames, and Poplar, West Ham, Shoreditch, Whitechapel and Stepney, north of the Thames, which had, somewhat earlier, taken a pounding. Mrs Phillips periodically reported with pride that 'Bermondsey had copped it', which served to remind us that things were certainly worse elsewhere. After our night of terror and the discomfiture of the loss of power supplies at home, things slowly returned to normal, largely thanks to Mum who was determined to restore the domestic cleanliness and neatness in which she took pride. We were no longer fed at the community rest centre where we had been sent after the bombing, as Mum did marvels with our rations, as cooking a Sunday lunch took most of the week's meat supply. Dad was back at work in the docks and on the Thames moving goods and food along the river in barges towed by tugs to and from the ships and warehouses lining the Thames from the estuary to the upper reaches of the Pool of London. We were never really seriously short of food because Dad had heeded the slogan 'Dig for Victory' and so we had become self-sufficient in fresh fruit and root crops but, in the meantime, the decision had been taken to send us to South Devon. Gwen's school, Haberdashers' Aske's, shared facilities with Teignmouth Grammar School where we had been given fee-paying places, so it was now simply a matter of finding a good billet in the town. We departed for Teignmouth where Gwen was to meet us to take us to our new home and our new school and where, for the first time in ages, we were to receive a good education, wearing the Teignmouth Grammar School blazer, tie and badge. Our schooling could now resume.

At the outset things started well; we went to live with Mr & Mrs Fraser who owned and ran Teignmouth's principal drapery store. Mr Fraser was also a Special Constable. They lived in an impressive terraced house in a tranquil and nice neighbourhood close to our new school. The trouble with these arrangements was that Alan and I had separate agendas; we wanted to return home to live with our parents who now faced the German onslaught without us. We felt as if we had betrayed our birthright by leaving home. However, not being entirely bereft of some common sense, we felt that this move to Devon could perhaps be put to our advantage in the short term. Alan even suggested, correctly as it turned out, that it was only a matter of time before Teignmouth was itself bombed. This could be our ticket home if we survived the bombing. Already Gwen had said that the adjacent towns of Exeter and Plymouth were under attack and that much damage and loss of life had ensued. Devon was as much of a target as London and the south-east.

So in the spring and summer of 1941 we fell in love with this attractive seaside resort. The Teignmouth Grammar School, for the time being anyway, proved to be just the place for us. We were never sure about the Fraser billet for a number of absurd reasons and so we foolishly agitated for a move. Such ingratitude was embarrassing and quite indefensible. Mr & Mrs Fraser were delightful as well as hospitable and caring. Why then did we want to move? I rather fear the explanation was the same as usual: our manic desire to return to London to defend our beloved Mayday Gardens. Although we didn't fully understand it the truth was more complex and our experience of school was the key to our behaviour.

Teignmouth Grammar School, founded twenty years earlier, rightly enjoyed much local admiration for its high academic standards and was situated in a central position, not far from the centre of town and the sea. We liked our new school friends, as well as the co-ed nature of the school, with the girls dressed in smart blazers and skirts. Obviously we were developing our pre-teen interest in girls but were still free from the sexual drive and guilt that was to come later. Our interest in girls developed slowly but never really displaced the war as our central interest until 1945. We had always admired our clever and attractive sister who was some nine years older than us and this, by extension, led us to be attracted to girls of a similar personality, character, and background. This was perhaps the beginning of a major fault line in our education as the onset of puberty constantly derailed our interest in learning. Girls were alluring creatures.

We both saw our first naked girl in the Frasers' shed at bottom of the garden where, with our encouragement, on several consecutive Saturdays, a twelve-year-old girl was willing to undress. Her nudity was stunning even though she was not fully nubile and, conveniently, she lived next door. Her impact though was seismic. Eric, the evacuee who lived next door, made a remark to the girl that none of us properly understood at the time. It was some years before we fully understood his somewhat lewd remark: he asked her 'whether he could plant his carrot in her garden'. She replied politely that her family had plenty of carrots, thank you very much.

We couldn't work out exactly why she would want to do this but it was all really innocent, yet much more interesting to us than the rules of grammar and arithmetic and, unsurprisingly, our homework also suffered. The following extract from page 80 of the school magazine in 1941 confirms this:

> Form 1 consists of twenty-two small, innocent looking little boys. But they are not as innocent as they look. 'The Williams' twins can never find any ink so that is why their homework is sometimes missing.'

Although we never rose above Form 1B we did get some grounding in English. It was never enough though because our stay at the school was to prove rather brief as, after only one and a half terms, we were on our way home again following, in part, from a silly incident with an inexperienced, but well meaning, schoolmaster who, thanks to us, lost control of his class one afternoon.

It was a hot day and our English lesson was, therefore, held outdoors and attended by some twenty little boys whose capacity to stay focused was, to say the least, limited. The events of that day are etched in my mind with the clarity of an Old Dutch master. During an English lesson when I found it difficult to stay alert, Alan fell into a deep sleep and slept quite peacefully for the hour allotted for this class. On the stroke of three, the form master gently tried to wake Alan by pushing his well-polished shoe against Alan's bottom and was greatly surprised when his sleeping pupil, sprang to life, grabbed his left leg and accidently brought him to the ground with a resounding thud. The class took this as a cue to start a riot and I, in a twin reflex action, jumped on the back of Mr Moss who was attempting to get to his feet. I caught him off balance, sending him to the ground again and then attempted the *coup de grâce* by jumping on him in a futile bid to hold him down to facilitate Alan's escape. This lamentable scene was witnessed by pretty well the entire lower school, including the girls of the Haberdashers' Aske's School, as the pupils changed class rooms between lessons. So to add to the spectacle Gwen, our elder sister, and her giggling girlfriends witnessed the escapade. With growing disbelief one girl said to Gwen, 'Isn't that your brother swinging on the back of Mr Moss?' 'No,' Gwen replied, 'I don't have a brother at that school, and if I did I'd be deeply ashamed of him.' We twins took to our feet and fled to the bushes to try to hide from our pursuers, two of the younger masters and three prefects, who eventually seized us and took us to the headmaster.

Mr Silverston the headmaster, normally a kindly man, viewed us both with some disdain. He declared that in twenty years of teaching he had never witnessed such mayhem and it was likely that we would be expelled before the end of term – in less than a month. He asked for an explanation of our conduct. The silence which followed was broken when I offered to make an apology to both our form master and to the school. I said that my brother hadn't intentionally pushed the schoolmaster and that I'd gone to his aid as an automatic response. I intoned in contrite manner, 'We both regret this temporary lapse in good manners.' Mr Silverston turned towards Alan and said 'What, boy, do you have to say about this disgraceful behaviour?' Alan solemnly echoed my apology. Mr Silverston then said, 'I don't believe either of you can give a credible explanation for what you did, you might have been emotionally upset by your experience of the Blitz, but the damage done to the school's reputation cannot be easily erased.' Mr Silverston didn't really expect to hear a credible explanation, so I said, 'Sir, this is what twins do when the other twin is in trouble – even though no such attack was, I now know, actually being made but Alan thought he was under assault.' 'Well,' said the headmaster, 'I will of course get Mr Moss' account of this regrettable episode but though you both speak well I detect an underlying weakness in your excuse to explain such intemperate conduct. I will of course be writing to your father about this.' We were then dismissed. On the way out I spotted Gwen standing by the door with Mr Moss. She politely entered the room and asked to see the headmaster as soon as possible. She said that she was responsible for us. Gwen told us later what happened and neither of us had good reason to doubt the accuracy of the account. She told the headmaster that we had been greatly affected psychologically by the bombing that had partly destroyed our London home and thus our bad behaviour could be best explained by the loss of our home leading to our sudden evacuation to Teignmouth. Gwen told Mr Silverston that her brothers' deepest wish was to get back home. Mr Silverston tartly replied, 'We can soon facilitate that!' At the time Gwen was carrying a number of heavy books, the sign of a serious, senior girl and Mr Silverstone noticed one of the books was a copy of E. H. Carr's book *The Twenty Year Crisis*. Gwen said she had yet to read it. 'Well,' said the headmaster, 'when you do read it you will have read one of the most important books published on collective security and why it failed to keep the peace.' He thanked her for speaking up for her brothers and he then presumably saw Mr Moss before seeing us again. Some twenty years later in 1961 Mr Moss gave his account of this episode when I was in Teignmouth to address the local branch of the United Nations Association on the future of arms control and disarmament. He was a delightful man who said that the whole incident was blown up out of all proportion and that, at the time, he had argued in our favour and that there was never any intention of expelling us from the school as it was not a serious matter.

So when we returned to Mr Silverston's study he was smiling. He said, in effect, that though our behaviour had been unacceptable, Mr Moss had spoken up for us and blamed himself for using the tip of his shoe to wake Alan up. 'So,' said the headmaster, 'by acting together as you did it was something like collective security, but I don't expect you to understand that remark.' 'Well Sir,' I replied, 'what we did was not really *collective security* as much as self defence because had it been *collective security* the whole class would have fallen on Mr Moss.' The room echoed with the headmaster's loud laughter as he instructed us to return to our classroom for a lesson on the work of the League of Nations.

The summer holidays now lay ahead and we were still unsure if we were to be expelled or not. Two events then impinged on our situation: the German invasion of Russia and the arrival in Britain of Hitler's deputy, Rudolph Hess, to negotiate an Anglo-German peace.

These events, in an extraordinary way, changed everything for us in Teignmouth as, curiously enough, they played a crucial part in our finding ourselves in the best evacuation billet we were ever to enjoy. Life was about to change in a totally unexpected way.

5

Hubris and Fate

The end of term approached and, as no action was taken against us, life at school passed quickly and pleasantly. Sports Day was well attended by parents and friends, the result, no doubt, of a slight surge in the population of the town in the mid-1930s.

We both took part in the Sports Day events including the running and egg-and-spoon races but we finished last in both those events since Alan and I were small for our age, although strong and willing to compete.

In Form 1B we were popular with other boys but found Mr Moss, who shared the teaching with Mr Wheeler, wary of us, for good reason, given our non-compliant influence and our attention span which was limited as well as selective. History and English were our favourite subjects and arithmetic the least liked. We felt we were trying to do better but this was not widely accepted as we were regarded as lazy and disorganised which was, of course, absolutely true.

Miss King, the music mistress, invited us to audition for a choir she was attempting to form. Duly flattered, we, with lots of other boys, crowded into the music room for the audition. We were told to stand with the small boys and girls, roughly of our age and size. Standing behind us were older boys and girls whose musical talents were already known to Miss King, and approved by a colleague of hers, Miss Preedy. Alan promptly failed his audition but I survived another week by miming to the music rather than actually singing. I was soon asked to leave the choir. So far we'd failed to succeed in anything! We took this setback, as with so many others, in good heart. Failure rather than success actually gave us the self-confidence to avoid serious schooling. If we were not up to it did that matter? Not to us, as Alan said to me, 'We twins will fail together but succeed individually.' We were 'the twins' with a mission to contribute to the war effort unreservedly. How our friends laughed at us for saying such things, yet envied our humour and acceptance of unabashed failure and all hoped that the war effort was going better.

The school was teeming with pupils as it was now somewhat enlarged by sharing accommodation with the Haberdasher's Girls' School from New Cross, which made us feel at home, if at times, homesick. Gwen, our sister, kept an eye on us especially in light of the infamous incident from whose consequences she had saved us. Or had she? Gwen invited us both to tea at a café in Shaldon, across the narrow stretch of water best approached by ferry from Teignmouth, to hear some good news from home. 'It was possible,' she said, 'that we might receive some news about us leaving the Fraser household if an alternative place could be found close to our school.' We wondered whether she had done the right thing to help us quit the Fraser house but it was now too late, the decision had been made.

Mrs Fraser was deeply offended by our lack of gratitude for all that she had done for us and was no doubt puzzled also by my sudden refusal to take the family dog, a wire-haired Terrier, for a walk along the sea front which I had done so often. I adored the dog but it had got into a rather fierce fight with a bigger dog so as a result I lost all confidence that

I could prevent the dog from fighting. His habit of fighting every other dog he encountered made taking him for a walk a nightmare especially along Teignmouth's splendid promenade.

We liked and respected the Fraser family but domestic tension and friction between them and us had reached boiling-point. Although it was silly and hurtful I had written several letters home critical of the way in which they fed us; for example we thought they topped up the milk with water as well as making very bad porridge which was too thick to eat. The Frasers' anxieties had also been raised by sporadic air attacks on Teignmouth, which caused the death of an old pupil at our school, Beatrice James, who was killed while on duty as a nurse in Teignmouth hospital. The Frasers were also worried about their son who was a trainee pilot in the RAF. The war was never far away. The invasion menace had not really receded.

We went to Shaldon to hear from Gwen about our new billet over tea and cakes. She told us that we were going to be interviewed by two rather formidable ladies, both of whom were retired hospital matrons. They lived in a rather big house close to our school and employed a number of servants as well as a gardener. One of the women, the elder of the two, was the daughter of a doctor and the other was a daughter of a senior naval officer. Neither had married and rumour had it that they had been engaged to men who had been killed in the First World War.

They had plenty of room for two evacuees. However, they had decided to interview six boys to see which two were the sort of children who would fit in to a middle-class household. Gwen thought, from what she had heard from her own headmistress who was on social terms with the two elderly ladies, that they would prefer boys around our age, rather than the teenagers.

Gwen also told us that she had heard from Dad that 22 Mayday Gardens had been partially repaired and that the roof was back on with the bedroom windows restored. Apparently Mum had taken a part-time job selling women's hats in an exclusive shop in Blackheath village and the bombing was less frequent and, to everyone's relief, the night-time bombing attacks were fewer in number.

However, the fear of invasion still persisted as we waited for Hitler to calculate his next move, which came on Sunday 22 June 1941, the day of our interview with the two upper-class ladies. This had to go well since we had burnt our bridges with the Fraser family. So our first encounter with the two ladies, Miss Smith and Miss Wilson, was overshadowed by the news that Britain now had an ally – Russia.

The afternoon of the interview duly arrived and we made our way up the gravel path to this large Edwardian house and rang the front doorbell. We were only days away from the start of our summer holidays and on the previous day our attempt to join the Air Training Corps had been turned down since we were too young, so our self-confidence was not high as we approached the house, which occupied a prominent position high above the town. Alan said to me that it was the kind of house we deserved to live in.

Dressed in our school uniform we entered the house through the front door which had had been opened by one of the servants and were ushered into the impressive entrance hall with high ceilings. We walked across a wooden floor bordered by indoor plants beneath walls hung with pictures in heavy frames and were shown into the study. Inside the two ladies sat at a large table in a room surrounded by bookshelves. Huge windows faced due south in the direction of the sea and the garden outside stretched beyond our vision.

A dark stained grandfather clock ticked away rather loudly throughout the ordeal of the interview. We were directed to sit on a wide wooden bench facing our interlocutors that creaked and groaned under our combined weight and threatened to tip us onto the highly polished floor. We were nearly overwhelmed by the apparent formality of the occasion, yet equally impressed that we were there at all.

The room was a cross between a surgery and an admiral's chart room but the books gave it an academic menace like that of a headmaster's study. We found this so completely intimidating that we knew we had to rise to the occasion and we did. We were at our duplicitous best: soon we had both these ladies openly acknowledging that we were their ideal evacuees! Moreover, Alan was able to tell them the dramatic news that Nazi Germany had invaded Russia and I weighed in with the strange business of Hess, who had flown to Scotland on the eve of Germany's attack on the USSR. Were these events related? Both ladies then looked astounded when I added that Hitler had chosen the 129th anniversary of Napoleon's Russian campaign to open his own offensive. Our sister Gwen, a budding historian, had actually pointed this out to us just before the dreaded interview. Gwen had also remarked that she hoped the German soldiers had good winter clothing because the Barbarossa campaign would almost certainly take more than eight to ten weeks to defeat even a depleted Russian Army. How right she was. The elder of the two ladies remarked to Alan that Stalin had purged the Red Army of its finest officers and now faced the formidable German Army, so the Soviets would do less well than the Allies envisaged. This conversation was well over our heads but we nodded sagely in agreement as if we were fully aware of its implications for Britain and Russia now locked in a titanic struggle against possibly the finest army the Germans had ever fielded.

The interview then started with a crucial question, 'What does your father do?' I replied that he was in the Royal Navy which was untrue at the time. The elder of the two ladies then asked what rank he was. I replied that he was a Captain. I delivered this sentence with the emphasis firmly on the past tense. Miss Wilson interjected, 'What does he do now?' I quickly responded with a blatant untruth that he was sadly drowned when his ship went down off the Norwegian coast. Both women looked startled, 'You poor boys,' they both exclaimed in unison. 'What of your poor mother? Where is she?' 'Still in London,' I said, 'where she worked at the Admiralty doing "hush-hush" work for Naval Intelligence.' There was a perceptible intake of breath. 'Do you come from a well established family?' one of them asked. 'Yes,' said Alan firmly, 'and we also have a sister whose school is evacuated to Teignmouth and which is now sharing part of the Grammar School.' 'How old is she?' came the reply. 'She's seventeen,' he said. Actually Alan was furious with me for saying that dad was dead and that our mother was working for Naval Intelligence. He glared crossly at me in obvious dissent.

Both ladies glanced at each other with a knowing look. 'We had a meeting with your headmaster yesterday,' the elder lady said, 'and he told us how your sister saved you both from certain expulsion.' We fell silent. Only the clock was heard. This would scupper us for certain I thought to myself as we were then told, somewhat brusquely, to leave the room and make our way to the kitchen for tea with the servants. Half an hour later both ladies appeared and said, 'Collect your things from the Frasers' and move in tonight.' We did.

Our new bedroom was very large with two beds but, for mutual comfort, we chose to sleep together for our first night in the house. So began our remarkable experience of how the 'other half' lived. Dad was not yet in the Navy despite what I had said, though in 1942 he did join a specially recruited flotilla of landing ships for the Dieppe raid. His contract was to serve as an Able Seamen in the so-called 'six months navy' or the 'Millionaire's Navy' as it was also known, who were the envy of the fleet as they were paid at trade union rates close to the pay of an officer. However Dad never took part in the Dieppe raid itself because he was pulled out of the operation in view of his age and because his commanding officer thought that he had already done his bit in the First World War. As for Mum she continued to work in her shop selling hats totally unaware of the 'hush-hush' work for the Admiralty which I had said she was doing. In the meantime, we settled down to our upper-class existence in the relative safety and charm of South Devon. It proved to be a salutary experience not least in revealing to us a great deal about the caste-like divisions, which disfigured the English middle class in the 1940s. Our new hosts had money and influence in abundance and certainly proved caring and generous to us in every respect. They also seemed to be aware that the old order was dying and that a fundamental shift in power and influence was likely to occur as a result of the war.

They were aware that a more egalitarian society was emerging from the womb of the old and this war was about to trigger massive social change. Alan already had an intuitive grasp of collectivist ideas, which had begun to take root in his mind. Indeed, 1941 turned out to be a watershed in British social history although we did not know this and could not have properly understood it.

The ladies were leading lights in the local community and tried to influence people by holding discussion meetings, which were restricted in number and agenda. We were, remarkably enough, allowed to attend the first part of these periodic proceedings by helping the parlour maid serve tea and cakes. Those attending were mainly senior officers of the three fighting services and the Home Guard and Civil Defence. This experience helped shape our world view. It extended our horizons beyond our thoughts of home in 22 Mayday Gardens, although I continued to maintain the fiction that we lived in a large house in Blackheath in extensive grounds.

Alan strongly urged me to tell the ladies the truth about Dad's supposed death and, wisely, I also sent a letter home to our parents about the unfortunate events at school to head off the headmaster's letter dealing with our misconduct. The details of my letter shocked our parents but the ladies seemed less surprised to hear the truth about Dad, since it then transpired they had friends at the admiralty who could find no trace of my father's alleged drowning. They were amused rather than irritated by my story as they had grown to like us and, having got our home address from the school, had already written to our father saying that they would be willing to adopt us if he would agree to us being sent to a naval school as his sons were in need of discipline. Which school was that? We had heard of Osborne on the Isle of Wight as a possible school but it had closed some years ago although we later found it had moved to Dartmouth, which was too close for comfort.

Apparently Dad had agreed in an exchange of letters with the ladies resulting in the idea that a naval school might be the only way to get us to take our schooling seriously. This was a bombshell. How could we prevent this from going any further? Surely our mother would never agree to this so I promptly wrote a letter to her saying that, as we loved both our parents dearly, how could she possibly agree to parting with us on a permanent basis, but I received no reply. Things were looking extremely menacing so we went post-haste to our sister. Gwen said that Dad had written to her to say that he would shortly come to Teignmouth to complete the agreement. We seemed done for – lock, stock and barrel.

We were never to be underestimated and our determination to return home was now a test of our resolve and native cunning. We composed a message worthy of Goebbels which read 'Home next week. All is forgiven, Love Alan and Geoffrey.' Our calculation was that this telegram would strengthen Mum's presumed opposition to the permanent loss of her dear boys and was, indeed, a master stroke since, little did we know, a near-tragedy had occurred which helped us out of a difficult situation. Mum had just escaped death in a road accident when she had been hit by an Army lorry travelling at speed, although it was several weeks before we actually knew of this serious incident.

In the meantime, we had reconciled ourselves to staying in Teignmouth since we had survived our possible expulsion from school. We had also survived the revelation of our tale of the supposed death of our father and had miraculously managed to keep the elderly ladies on side. The weather that August was good and the strong scent of summer pervaded the garden where several local cats slept in the shade of the subtropical plants. Even to this day the smell of roses and hydrangeas can transport me to Devon with its distinctive reddish soil under the undulating fields. We were happy and relaxed there with the added excitement that the Germans were now attacking Teignmouth in isolated raids on targets of opportunity. We cycled along coastal roads surrounded by barbed wire and newly built anti-tank obstacles that were strategically placed to block the invader.

This was where we imagined the troops of the Spanish Armada would have landed just as the Germans now planned to do so. A school friend invited us to come and help feed the chickens on his father's farm and we were rewarded with a couple of eggs for our efforts to augment our rations, which had been reduced again as British merchant shipping loses increased. We had a long talk with the cook and the pantry maid as to how it was that they were able to provide us with such tasty food on the rations we received. Alan asked whether there was one ration for the poor and another for the rich. Both girls thought not; they believed that the rations were the same for all. But they did say that people with money could dine out in the restaurants that were not subject to rationing. We were surprised to hear this as we had heard that the pubs were selling weak beer and dog-eared sandwiches. The more expensive restaurants in Teignmouth, however, were still doing a good trade as elderly holidaymakers still came to the resort, war or no war.

The youngish cook, whom we adored, told us that the weekly rations would have been sufficient for a single helping in a pre-war household. She said that people could manage on these weekly rations which only amounted to a shilling's worth of meat, one ounce of cheese, four ounces of bacon or ham, two ounces of jam or marmalade plus two ounces of butter provided the supplies got through. We spoke to Gwen about this and she said that the bacon ration was actually fixed at a level higher than the average pre-war consumption and that people were doing well on the balanced rations drawn up by dietary experts working for the Ministry of Food, so obesity actually declined as people adapted to the war economy.

I distinctly remember being offered eggs and bacon for breakfast throughout our stay in this large house. So did this explain why our elegant hostesses ate very little for breakfast when we were there? The plain loaf of bread became an in-demand delicacy for all of us and even to this day a slice of bread is always acceptable. Of course vegetables and potatoes were never in short supply in Devon. We thrived and our strength and weight, for a couple of ten-year-olds, was about the average for boys from a prosperous background. Also we noticed that the local fish and chip shop never seemed to be short of supplies or customers: we often went there on our way back to our temporary home after an afternoon spent at the pictures with pocket money to spare given the generous weekly stipend of 2s 6d each, which we received from our over-generous hosts. We secretly saved some of this money, however, for the day when we made a bid to get back to Mayday Gardens. Alan, very typically, saved more than I did as well as spending less on sweets and custard pies. Saving money was made infinitely easier in a wartime economy where consumption of goods and services fell dramatically.

In relation to our weekly visits to the cinema, the film that made the biggest impression on us was *Night Train to Munich* with Rex Harrison acting the part of a British spy. We found this film dramatic as well as funny because of the two quintessentially English characters: Charters and Caldicott, played by Basil Radford and Norton Wayne. They gave a brilliant performance as cricket-loving duffers caught in the drama of the outbreak of war on a train to Munich. Charters and Caldicott soon became our role models, who awakened our interest in county cricket and the unrelated, but slightly raffish, work of military espionage.

The war was getting nastier by the day and was dominated by the Battle of the Atlantic and the continued threats of invasion in the first half of 1941, a threat that persisted well into 1942. Being now able to read and write to a reasonable standard, our reading habits improved and we read short history books as well as newspapers and periodicals such as the popular *Picture Post* but rarely read comics.

We even developed a sense of irony greatly assisted by Gwen's sisterly advice to digest and memorise what we saw and read with a sceptical eye. We memorised some of the wartime slogans and later in the war, we enjoyed the BBC radio shows like *ITMA* [It's That Man Again] with Tommy Handley. One weekend Gwen asked us to interpret for her one of the most famous wartime slogans then on bill boards and buses which read; '*Your Courage, Your Cheerfulness, Your Resolution, Will Bring Us Victory*', 'Who,' she said, 'were the us and who were the we?' Alan thought 'we were us' and 'us were we'.

Four days later, when we'd just finished breakfast, Gwen arrived to see both of our kindly hosts and we were told to leave the room and shortly afterwards, Gwen told us to pack our bags and be ready to catch the late afternoon train to Paddington! We were going home and so, with tears shed all round by the entire household, we took our leave of Teignmouth. Gwen had absolutely no idea why this sudden, almost brutal, departure was necessary, so naturally on the train journey thoughts of going home to our parents were uppermost in our minds as it still wasn't clear to us why we had had to leave in such a hurry. Clearly our unreal existence on the coast of Devon had come to an end and it would be twenty years before I returned to this delightful resort.

The tragedy, in the long term, was that we lost contact with these kindly and intelligent women who did so much for us. Despite visits to Teignmouth long after the war by both my brother and myself we could find no trace of them or even of their house and we cannot now even be certain of their names so the eponymous names cited in this chapter are those we think we remember. We were also close to the housekeeper and her assistants whom we adored. They looked after us both so well even helping with our homework while speaking to us in their soft Devonshire accents which, in private, we would then imitate.

It was a lovely household and so leaving was a wrench. When asked if we were still homesick we would reply that we were because we wanted to go home to keep the Nazi invaders out of Mayday Gardens. In fact the truth was that we greatly missed our parents.

6

Home at Last

As we approached London, Alan looked wistfully out of the window for the red London Transport buses as the train threaded its way through Outer London to Paddington station. Gwen, who would shortly return to Teignmouth, peered intently at the bomb damage sustained by the houses and shops of suburbia. I enjoyed the reassurance of familiar sights and sounds; I liked the very smell of London and its unending urgent bustle. Gwen remarked that 'when a man is tired of London he is tired of life'. 'Who said that?' I asked 'Samuel Johnson,' she replied. 'He's dead right,' said Alan.

My attention was drawn to the trams that took us noisily through Elephant and Castle, New Cross, Lee Green, Eltham, and then home to Mayday Gardens and reminded us that London remained, in our eyes, the centre of the world. How had London survived without us? Our childish perspective rested on the simple things that go with returning home at last: yet why now? The explanation soon emerged.

Dad was waiting at the tram stop in Well Hall Road as we alighted. Gwen got off first and we boys followed quickly, clutching our heavy bags with the help of the tram conductor. We had noticed how everyone we saw looked tired and strained. Dad also looked older, his face exuded anxiety and uncertainty, and he quickly got to the point.

'Your mother has a broken leg and is recovering from severe concussion having been run over by an Army lorry. She wants you home to help with her recovery. Please make every effort to help her.' We agreed to be considerate and helpful so, still in a state of shock from this news, we walked slowly along the familiar path home to Mayday Gardens, via Broad Walk, and the 10-foot wall behind which was the Royal Herbert Military Hospital. When we reached the house we saw immediately that the roof was back on and our windows were back in. Across the road, about 60 yards ahead, a huge gap was visible between the houses on both side of the road where the land mine had stuck. Only the outlines of the former foundations of the houses remained, but most of the debris had gone and subsequently, in 1943, a vast water tank for use in the face of an expected firebomb attack would be installed. This NFS water tank was to become our playground; it was almost our private lake.

We entered the front door of our house and found Mum sitting in the dining room with her left leg covered in plaster. She rose to her feet and kissed us on the cheek with the smile we knew so well. 'Can you walk?' I asked. 'Yes,' she said, 'with the use of a stick and the plaster will come off next month.' She still looked young and attractive but obviously very tired.

The house was immaculate just as it was before the land mine struck although, despite constant polishing, Mum's piano, still pitted with glass from the bomb damage, never regained its pristine condition. The musical instrument itself, however, was still perfect according to the piano tuner who came once very three months to tune it. The back garden had gained an additional brick shelter – the Morrison shelter. This gave light cover for four to six people and was equipped with bunks and an escape hatch at the back should its occupants wish to get out in a hurry. A quick trip round the garden revealed that Dad had been 'Digging for Victory' as part of the lawn had been dug up to grow vegetables in addition to the flower beds on either side. We therefore enjoyed the fruits of his labours as the Battle of the Atlantic took its toll on the food supplies.

Over supper that evening the full story of our 'adoption' by our Teignmouth hostesses was revealed and it was apparently a close-run thing as the idea had been taken seriously by Dad, although Mum had regarded it with marked disfavour despite saying that the idea did make some sense. It also transpired that our parents had a fallback plan for our future in the event of their death through German action. The original plan included either Aunt Ada or Aunt Dorrie taking responsibility for us so that we would be brought up together with Gwen living with either one or the other of the maternal aunts as circumstances permitted. When the Teignmouth plan had unfolded in the early summer, Dad had thought that, in the event of his or Mum's death, the wealthy spinsters in Devon would provide for our future especially in the light of their commitment to send us to the disciplined environment of a Royal Naval public school. Mum saw the logic of this but instinctively opposed it and she remained convinced that the best option was to keep her children in the family since her sisters were only too anxious to have us in the face of disaster. However, now that we were home the Teignmouth plan was dead in the water and we twins would stay together at home in London while Gwen would rejoin her evacuated school in Teignmouth at the end of the holidays. Alan and I were relieved and reassured by this strategy but markedly surprised by how close we came to being legally transferred to the upper classes. To be born poor was one thing but to be transferred to the upper division was another. As Alan said, 'they could never turn his red blood blue'. Alan saw class as the basic fault line in British politics, but I thought that the war had brought people together and had resulted in the unforced mixing of the classes. The war I felt would bring lasting social change.

Our poor performance at school had left my father depressed and Alan possibly dyslexic but for the next few days we searched for our friends, John Bray, Harry Savage and Barry Earps, but soon discovered that only John had returned home by 1942. Perhaps he had never actually left at all but had lived for a few months with his relatives in various parts of London. He was delighted to see us and we all set about reconstructing our lives as best we could. This took on a new urgency for us, as it became the basis for us to begin to make a real, or perhaps imaginary, contribution to the war effort. Naturally enough though, sending us back to school seemed to be the major parental priority but Alan and I had other ideas despite their plan to enrol us at the South East London Emergency Secondary School, which was based in Red Lion Lane, Shooters Hill, in Woolwich. However, as this could not be arranged immediately, we went *pro tem* to a local school in Haimo Road, Eltham.

Alan, John and I wanted to plant a tree in Jack Woods to mark the death of Peter, the teenage boy killed in the Mayday Gardens land mine attack. John filled in the details of Peter's last moments on earth in chilling detail but how he had come by this version of events he never fully disclosed. His account did, however, accord with eyewitness evidence provided by survivors on that terrible night. Peter was sitting with his huge St Bernard dog in the dining room of his house facing the French windows that looked out to the cemetery at the back. The German bombers had been overhead for a while before they dropped the huge land mine – actually a sea mine – which had floated down, penetrating the room and killing Peter's entire family. Nine or more people were in fact killed that night because members of the Home Guard had seen the parachute carrying the bomb and thought it was either a German pilot who had bailed out or, more likely, a German agent floating down so they too died as the bomb blew them to kingdom come when they rushed towards it.

John Bray's new motto was 'do not be in such a hurry to meet your maker': his somewhat mawkish approach to life made him a sardonic and amusing friend in the face of danger. He even suggested that many of the dead found in Mayday Gardens had been buried in the cemetery before the war. It was a somewhat macabre account but it may have been accurate because so many skeletons were scattered over a wide area. It was an awful business.

We now prepared ourselves to contribute to the war effort at last by initially joining the Army Cadets and later the Air Cadets, which was the most we thought we could achieve at our age unless the war itself went on for another decade. In the event the war did last long enough for all three us to have a role, which went beyond the Cadets when, in 1944, we joined the National Fire Service as messengers, but that was way ahead.

Meanwhile, as summer passed into autumn and winter, the strategic position of Britain was to be transformed in a dramatic way that would immediately impinge on all of us. America's entry into the Second World War was as sudden and dramatic as the earlier Nazi invasion of Russia had proved to be. We heard the news about the Japanese attack on the US fleet at Pearl Harbor from the BBC and we pondered upon its significance for Britain and wondered whether or not it would mean American forces coming to fight over here, as Britain certainly needed their support if Europe was to be liberated.

Now back at school, our preoccupation centred on the Christmas holidays although, in the six months or more since our return from Teignmouth, our private thoughts were dominated by our experience there where we had learnt to read and had been encouraged to think. We had enjoyed the hospitality, kindness, and the respect of local people as did so many evacuees in a country torn by war but not yet divided by it. We had never wanted to leave home and only the war had made it necessary, but we were part of a mass movement of the young whose lives would forever be defined by it. Gwen, our greatly admired sister, took the view that little harm, if any, had been inflicted upon us by the great disruption of war and that we would soon catch up on our school work once we were ready to exert ourselves. This, however, was not something we wanted to do as, in fact, our return to London proved to be the opportunity for us to refocus on the war to the exclusion of all else.

Our grasp of what was now happening in the waging of this necessary war urgently required us to reassemble our mock battlefield on top of the Anderson shelter on a much grander scale. We possessed a vast army of lead soldiers who we had been mobilising since war had been declared and, in our bedroom, we hung maps showing the fluctuating fortunes of the war. This was now being fought in two theatres: in Russia and in South-East Asia/the Pacific, although the second front in Western Europe did not open until June 1944 with the D-Day landings. Our geographical knowledge was limited so we concentrated our thoughts on the European theatre of war. Therefore in our war games in the garden, weather permitting, we set about defeating the Germans and the Japanese simultaneously. Clausewitz had said that war was simple but that the simplest things in their execution were difficult.

We both had lost our fear of Nazi agents lurking in the woods and hiding in suburban houses, clandestinely sending radio messages to Berlin. This was not because we no longer believed that Nazi agents were active in London, especially in Woolwich with its military academy and huge military ordnance factory – the Royal Arsenal – which produced bombs and shells for the three fighting forces, but because we now attached greater importance to the early liberation of France rather than to our desperate search for spies. It was by no means certain that Britain would win the war, for we had considerable anxieties about the Suez Canal and Rommel's Afrika Corps, which represented a formidable threat to British military prowess. Alan started to take an interest in the Russian front, looking intently at maps as the Germans advanced inexorably into the Soviet heartland. Our vocabulary now included references to places which few of our school friends seemed to know of or were interested in – like Smolensk, Kiev and Moscow. We were concerned that the momentum of the German advance around Leningrad would knock Russia out of the war as the German attack on Moscow had induced panic in that city with the Soviet government about to flee. It all seemed to us so horribly familiar and inevitable that Russia would be defeated, as had France, Belgium, and the Low Countries in 1940. But we underestimated the nature of the Soviet regime and its brutal determination to survive as, on our birthday, 29 November, the Russian Army retook Rostov and within weeks Zhukov's counter-offensive was underway.

Alan solemnly told me as we played with our toy soldiers, that fighting in the cruel conditions of a Russian winter was as far from the warmth and comfort of our battlefield map room in our bedroom as could be imagined – he was certainly right. The BBC gleefully reported that the German retreat from Moscow was underway. We listened to every BBC bulletin and to as many reports as we could manage. But in the run up to Christmas in early December, our favourite date in the calendar for numerous undeserved gifts, there was bad news! Dad and Mum had failed to secure a chicken for Christmas Day so we were to have rabbit instead, a dish which I particularly disliked, having discovered that the rabbit was really a species of rodent. We urged our parents to make a renewed search for a chicken for our Christmas table. Then, a few days before the dreaded arrival of the rabbit, Alan and I were in the garden reequipping our toy soldiers deployed on top of the air-raid shelter, with reinforcements supplied by Harry Savage and John Bray, when a huge chicken waddled into the garden. This fat bird seemed happy with life and it crowed loudly as only a cockerel can as it searched for food. Where it had come from was to us less important than where were we going to put it once we had killed it. Yet the curious creature appeared unafraid and friendly and our desire to kill it diminished somewhat despite John Bray thinking that we should seize it and break its neck. We had no idea how this might be done, or by whom, so we rushed into the house to tell Dad that our Christmas dinner was walking around the back garden. He came out, flanked by Mum, who became anxious about the fate of the bird as it quietly continued strolling around, pecking at the detritus of twigs and leaves piled neatly at the bottom of the garden. 'Surely,' she said, 'someone nearby must own it. They've probably been fattening it up for the table. If we kill it then it's theft. We should have nothing to do with it.' 'Alfred,' she said, 'shoo it away in the direction of next door,' but, as our neighbours had duly appeared on the scene, we thought that the fate of the chicken was sealed. There were now no fewer than seven people chasing the creature including two men with murderous intent.

This chicken, however, proved to be no willing victim and valuing its life ran into the garden of the house on the side, disappearing as quickly as it had arrived and for years afterwards Alan and I speculated about this incident, which was so unreal since the appearance of a chicken in our garden raised the question of possible divine intervention. The possibility of this unlikely event was greatly strengthened in our febrile minds when, out of the blue, Dad announced that he'd managed to get a chicken for Christmas which was large enough to feed four or five of us for several days. Was this bird the one that had appeared in our garden?

We boys with others of our acquaintance, though not John and Harry our immediate neighbours, were about to break up for the Christmas holidays. Our recollections of Haimo Road School are virtually non-existent, except for the memory of a short tram journey to school each day and our return home for lunch as the school did not provide food which we thought edible and so going home for lunch was decidedly preferable to taking sandwiches to eat in class.

The truth was that after Teignmouth, and before our next secondary school, this school proved to be a miserable experience situated as it was in an area of poor dilapidated housing, just off several semi-deserted roads leading to Eltham on one side and Lee on the other. We failed to make any close friends there and were constantly harassed by the bigger boys, who frightened us more than the German bombers, which were still relatively active over London.

Yet we knew that in the New Year we would be switching schools if we secured a place at the South East London Emergency Secondary School. This would mean quite a long walk to school through Castle Wood and then up the Shooters Hill Road to an area surrounded by solid houses and trees high above the Military Academy. This Emergency School was comprised of the Colfe's Grammar School, the Roan School and several other excellent schools, all of which were operating with a growing number of pupils who, like us, had returned home as the German war machine turned its attention elsewhere when the Russian Front had been opened earlier in the summer.

We faced an entrance exam which, if successfully negotiated, could lead to a scholarship. Although we, quite inexplicably, passed this exam and gained entry to the school, we failed to be awarded scholarships and so were fee-paying pupils with the concomitant financial burden falling on Dad. Luckily his earnings were high as Thames lightermen were well paid with the addition of lots of overtime as the Port of London became the powerhouse of the growing war economy. We lived well, the New Year promised much and we boys looked forward to going to a new school. People were now contemplating what would happen once Britain had defeated Germany.

In fact from late 1941, a wider preoccupation with the problems of social reform had become apparent at all levels of society. Alan took greater interest in social reform than I did; he appeared to know about the '1941 Committee' of upper-class liberals and socialist intellectuals which later proved to be the forerunner of the Commonwealth Party, founded in 1943, and which set out a new agenda for reform. We were, Alan told me, echoing the views of our Teignmouth hosts, on the threshold of a new world in which the theories and practices of the past were dead. He insisted that this reform would be backed by the trades unions and the Labour Party, and that throughout the year, in fact since May, a specialist committee had been working on proposals to put into effect a comprehensive social insurance system for the entire nation when the war ended. This was in fact the 1942 Beveridge Report.

I was astonished by Alan's grasp of the detail; he even mentioned the name of William Beveridge, who, it seemed to me, was a much lesser figure than Churchill or the Chiefs of Staff. Alan's growing interest in politics began to overshadow his interest in military matters, while mine remained focused on these. Yet Alan was able to link the two converging areas of policy and of war and demonstrated this in heckling a communist speaker in Beresford's Square, Woolwich, about Stalin's Russia. He asked the speaker to explain why the war against Germany had once just been a capitalists' war but was now, since Russia's entry into the conflict, a war worth fighting. He received a somewhat convoluted reply that the class war was but the conflict leading to a real social revolution. The Soviet Union therefore had to be saved from defeat by the British people.

7

The Long Slog

Hitler's promised invasion of Britain never materialised, so we boys never did see a German soldier or agent on British soil, although we did see some Italian prisoners-of-war in 1944, but in 1942 the outlook for us suddenly seemed more tedious and dull than dramatic. The war for us had taken on a new image – the battle on the home front. The best we could do was to join the Army Cadets but that was not officially possible until we were fourteen years of age, so in the meantime we decided to develop our boys own 'Home Guard' on a much more ambitious scale than hitherto known. We would aim for three platoons, or even more, armed with weapons which we ourselves would develop and deploy. We energetically recruited the potential rank and file from our own school who were mostly from our own age group as well as from the elementary schools in our neighbourhood. Recruits could be no younger than nine and no older than twelve and were expected to pass a written or oral test before being admitted to our force, which was called 'The Shooters Hill Boys Own Home Guard Unit' and was inspired by the Roman Legions who had used this road as they made their way to London. The test was simple and basic and the score gained determined your rank. We asked the following questions: 'Why are we at war with Germany?' and 'What action would you take to tackle an invader trying to gain entry to your home or school?' Even more relevantly we asked, 'Do you promise to obey our lawful commands when on active duty and promise not to run away from the enemy?' We recruited twenty-five boys of whom only twelve could be relied on to turn up for duty at short notice. No member of the 'Unit' was expected to have his orders overruled by parents and never by school teachers or the local clergy except in the most exceptional circumstances.

Once recruits had passed their basic training, which was spread over no fewer than four consecutive Saturdays between ten in the morning and twelve noon, they could take their staff promotion exam based on the questions posed above and on an interview which determined their military rank. Once this process had been completed members of the force would then be kitted out with their uniforms and imitation rifles and machine guns, which John Bray brilliantly made from items rescued from the numerous bomb sites and dumps. Later we made part of an old motor mower into a make believe artillery piece which was manned by three boys in a support role.

The local boys loved their uniforms which were made from a large consignment of coarse, thick pyjamas sent by the Australians for the use of evacuee children in the winter. However, the material had proved so rough to wear that this particular consignment had finished up in a bombed-out building, from whence we boys had retrieved it. The Khaki coloured material, which we wore adorned with real badges of rank purchased from the numerous military retailers in Woolwich and Eltham, looked very smart indeed when washed and ironed. We were in fact much better dressed than the real soldiers in their somewhat unkempt battle fatigues.

I was the commanding officer with the rank of Captain and three actual 'pips' on each shoulder and Alan and John were the Lieutenants, with Alan acting as an Adjutant and John as the training and education officer. We had two full staff-sergeants, three corporals, and a growing number of lance-corporals. They all helped us maintain what little order we could achieve amongst the rebellious ranks. We drew up a short training manual covering battlefield tactics and drill both on and off the battlefield and everyone was expected to attend ceremonial parades when ordered. These parades were held in Broad Walk alongside the Military Hospital before or after the real army conducted its full military burial parades.

Discipline was supposed to be tight. When on parade we marched three to a line with the officers and NCOs on the flanks and the commanding officer in front. Later we even had a small band with instruments mostly made from material picked up from bomb sites as well as some abandoned trumpets and drums found in bombed out dwellings. These made an unbelievable cacophony which was beyond the endurance of those with sensitive ears or any knowledge of music. Alan personally recruited three thirteen-year-old boys and one overweight girl for wrestling and unarmed combat, but our great achievement was that we were noticed by the indulgent adults which whetted our ambition. So by 1943 we had even built a mock-up of a German fighter, which the police told us to destroy, and a self-made early-warning detector device for a more precise and up-to-the-minute warning of an imminent air raid. Sadly enemy action actually caused the death of two of our special reservists while they were off duty asleep in their beds during a night air raid and so we offered the bereaved parents a military funeral for their boys, but in both cases they refused our offer saying it would be an insult to the British Army.

We needed a permanent HQ and we found it in a large deserted house at the top of Shooter's Hill called *The Limes* which, today, has been replaced by post-war flats. The house had its downside as some of our younger members refused to enter it because they believed it to be haunted. The house was once an elegant Victorian villa built for the well-known Jay family but it was now empty and near collapse. This made it quite dangerous with the greatest danger lurking in the cellar, which had been used as laboratory in earlier days by a chemist. Chemicals lay on the floor in bottles disturbed only by the infestation of rats that ran through the entire house with alarming rapidity. When it rained the building flooded as torrents of water flowed down the rickety staircase pouring into the deserted rooms below. The rooms were in fact very spacious with high ceilings providing plenty of light. The house was now simply abandoned and was almost beyond repair so it proved to be an ideal place to play our war games during foul weather.

Our new school in Red Lion Lane was at the bottom of the road which dipped steeply down from Shooter's Hill. Almost half way up this road was *The Limes*, our headquarters, which was ideal for our military operations and after-school training sessions. School work inevitably took second place to our self-defined war work and our form master accused us of forming nothing less than a gang of unruly boys engaged in protracted mischief. He wasn't far wrong as we had personally banned homework in the national interest!

The school was unusual as it was formed from several well-established grammar and secondary schools with a longer lineage than Teignmouth Grammar, which actually celebrated its twentieth anniversary during our brief stay there. Each of these schools had had a scholastic reputation in their own right now somewhat diminished by their wartime amalgamation but, even so, we were faced with the prospect of homework in all the basic subjects, whose mysteries still failed to arouse our interest. The only stimulants we sought were war related: collecting shrapnel, watching the night sky for searchlight activity or, on moonlit nights, for German bombers that were still coming over.

At home our concerns turned towards what we ate. Mum proved adaptable and took note of what the Ministry of Food wrote so we enjoyed substitute dishes such as Woolton Pie consisting of vegetables and potatoes, which was certainly tasty. A plain loaf of bread was still delivered daily with bottled milk arriving on the doorstep pretty much everyday. The slim weekly ration, and other foods on a points-based system, made for a rather limited choice but a balanced diet was assured in most households. This was fortunate because we were growing up and our bodies needed the nutritional food which, in the main, was provided efficiently even though there were some shortages from time to time. Rationing as a system worked and we just got used to the endless queues. We boys would join Mum for the daily shop during the school holidays and, although she seemed to enjoy shopping, this perhaps also reflected her desire to get out of the house everyday. Mum said that some shopkeepers had their favourite shoppers and kept back some supplies for them, which were often hidden beneath the counter and sold with a nod and a wink. The food at school was atrocious and so we used to sneak out to the local fish and chip shop. There was also a small café halfway up the Shooter's Hill Road, opposite the local church and Castle Wood, where we could occasionally get a sandwich or a sausage roll served by the glamorous daughters of a large Irish family. These girls were strikingly attractive and so, unsurprisingly, the café had a clientele of young soldiers and teenage boys hoping to ask them out. We already knew how to flirt and yet these girls were totally unattainable; at least that's what we thought.

One evening, late in 1942, Alan met Harry Savage who told him confidentially that Britain had a secret device which allowed the RAF to detect German bombers as they approached their targets inland. Alan said that it was tied up with the 'Biggin Hill' experiment. Later, when telling me about it, just before we went to bed, Dad's ears pricked up since the RAF station was situated close to Westerham. This it turned out had been Mum and Dad's favourite spot for never-disclosed sentimental reasons. Before the war, Dad had bought several acres of land there for £20 only to see the land requisitioned by the Air Ministry without being able to secure any compensation and so Dad confirmed, in his loud booming voice, that there had long been rumours about work being done there on the use of radio signals for defensive purposes. He said that the Air Ministry had installed some kind of device as early as 1936, whereby it was possible to locate aircraft by the use of radio waves. This invention, we later learnt after the war was over, was developed by Robert Watson-Watt, the Head of Radio Research at the National Physical Laboratory.

Both Alan and I were all ears since Paul Packman, the boy with whom we were initially evacuated in 1939, seemed to also know of it through his father's pre-war trips to the coast, when he had seen aerial towers erected near Dover. The rumour mill, via Mr and Mrs Phillips who still lived next door, also had confirmed that similar towers were to be found at places as far apart as Rye on the Sussex coast and Ventnor on the Isle of Wight where they always took their family holidays. Mr Phillips, a lorry driver of unblemished character, was well informed on these matters since he drove regularly across Kent, Sussex and Hampshire. All this talk of radio waves, which could determine the direction and height of an aircraft some 75 miles from a radar station, inspired us to develop our own early warning system for our boys in the special Boys Own Home Guard Unit, but before we could turn our minds to how best to develop such a system the war once again dominated our thinking.

The strategic situation for Britain had worsened in 1942 when the BBC reported the Japanese invasion of Burma and the seizure of Rangoon in early March. This cut the legendary Burma Road and forced the Allies across the Chindwin to the borders of India. News of this sent us scurrying to our atlas, supplied by Gwen from her growing number of books and papers, to see where this unfolding drama was taking place. We both knew that Hong Kong had had to surrender to the advancing Japanese over and above the earlier loss of Singapore, which had been a crushing blow to Britain's prestige. Apparently the British commander, Lieutenant General Percival, had ordered the surrender of his 85,000 British, Australian, and Indian troops to a Japanese general with the name of Yamashita. John Bray always emphasised the 'Shita' when speaking of this disaster: he possessed a colourful vocabulary of expletives. As John Bray's father, a regular soldier who had served in Singapore pre-war, said by quoting Mr Churchill, 'in the long history of British military action there is no more dismal chapter than the fall of Singapore'. John banged on about this for weeks on end and as a result we all went to school with our heads bowed and our spirits low. Worse was to follow when by the end of April it was reported that the Japanese had completed the conquest of central Burma. Also the news from the deserts of North Africa was downright depressing as Rommel stormed Tobruk and crossed the Egyptian frontier in 1942. All this, however, renewed our determination to prepare our boys' own forces for battle. The thrust of our training was how best to protect our platoon against the German Air Force, which was necessary because we were commanding troops who cried and deserted their posts on hearing the air-raid warning when on duty. Winning this war was indeed looking unpromising until, suddenly, in November, came the stunning news of the successful battle at El Alamein – the first real British success since the Battle of Britain. This victory was somewhat tempered by the news of the German encirclement of Stalingrad which added to Alan's despondency in particular. We therefore decided to change the unit's tactics away from territorial defence and towards passive rather than active defence. The three of us, Alan and John and myself, thought we would now develop an early warning system to enable us to alert our neighbours and our own unit to imminent air attack. In the meantime we turned our attention towards building a long-range bomber made from the rubbish collected from bomb sites in order to inflict strategic damage on German bases in Europe. We reasoned that defence and attack were different sides of the same coin. Yet how could a single homemade bomber, even if we could get it airborne, make a real difference to the war? Not before time we reconsidered where we stood in relation to the war itself. Playing games had got us nowhere.

This review changed our thinking completely and we now decided we would all join a real outfit such as the Army Cadets since our childish games had failed to provide a basis for any real part in the war which Britain appeared to be losing. We decided, therefore, that we, and the senior boys in our fighting unit, should defect to the Army Cadets or the Air Training Corps. It's difficult to recall why we suddenly decided to do this but perhaps the truth was that our hormones were kicking in and so our interest in the war was no longer centre stage, although we were not interested, as were others, in tobacco, drink, petty crime, or violent behaviour. We turned towards contemporary music, girls, and fun. We became less serious, although we had never been in any way conformist, as we began to see the error of our ways. This did not extend to preventing us from playing truant in order to escape from the tedium of lessons. We thought nothing of taking a detour on our way to school to help clear up bomb damage or help elderly people whose homes were exposed to the elements as a result of the bombing. We would help them put up government supplied cellophane windows and it was these local community activities that took the priority over school work. I do not recall a single occasion where someone in authority ever said, 'Why are you not at school?' though school inspectors were supposed to be on the lookout for truants since truancy had become a major social problem.

Around this time Alan and I noticed that there were men and women in semi-military uniforms who were apparently volunteer members of the Observer Corps. Members were drawn from across the country from among those who had a flair for aircraft recognition and the Corp developed highly sophisticated ways of estimating the height of incoming aircraft. I later learnt that there were 30,000 observers and 1,000 observation posts, each with a grid map, a height estimator, a telephone, coloured map markers, and tea-making facilities. Little did this vast organisation, scattered across the country as a backup for radar, know of our activities perched on the top of the derelict building, *The Limes*. Our activities there remained one of the best-kept secrets of the war even if not quite so 'hush-hush' as the so-called Enigma codes, which having been deciphered were now supplying accurate information on the German order of battle as they prepared to launch major raids against British targets. This, of course, remained top secret for years. Our amateur observation post worked on a shoestring using a make-do kit assembled from spare parts, sheeting, and several rolls of newspaper attached to a hoop about the size of a large and inverted orchestral drum. Once put in position, this could pick up sounds from several miles away. If the wind wasn't blowing we became adept at telling the difference between the sound of a tram leaving Woolwich or Eltham – a distance in either direction of less than three miles. While the knowledge of where the trams were was not vital to the war effort it was possible, on a dry and noiseless day, for us to pick up the distinctive sound of the standard twin-engine bombers, the Heinkel 111 and the Dornier 17, flying up the Thames from as far away as Gravesend or Dartford. We trained our ears to pick up the sound of Spitfires and Hurricanes at a similar distance and fine tuned our primitive equipment to detect the Messerschmitt 109. Yet a heavy raid would invariably drown out our simple detection system making the roar of aircraft sound like distant thunder. Our device was eventually struck by lightning in a violent storm after which we were afraid to use it. Our inventions belonged to the rich traditions of Fred Karno's army. It also demonstrated to Alan and me that our mundane technological efforts would be unlikely to have any impact on winning the war. Our various improvisations were not going to achieve the liberation of Europe so we had to be more practical.

We scoured the bomb sites to collect mirrors of all shapes and sizes, providing they had been abandoned by their owners, as we were intending to build an entirely new weapon which would direct the power of the sun at our opponent to completely confuse him when he was most vulnerable.

Our own 'R & D' brought rapid and unexpected results but was so simple and dangerous that we had to abandon it because, during the experimental phase, we inadvertently caused several fires in both Jack Wood and Castle Woods which necessitated the attendance of the NFS.

However, we kept the biggest mirror in which, in due course, we installed on the roof of *The Limes* to direct the beams skywards in a bid to destroy low-flying enemy aircraft.

We also boasted to Gwen about our new weapon and its capacity to start fires. Alan claimed that if a German plane flew low enough over *The Limes* we could bring it down by igniting its fuel tanks through the use of concentrated sunshine. Gwen scornfully suggested that while this was possible the use of mirrors to cause fires was far from new. Fire had been a part of warfare since time immemorial, so she reminded us of the fate of the Roman fleet when it attempted to invade Syracuse in Sicily in 21 BC. Archimedes positioned bronze mirrors directing sunlight on the invading fleet so setting it alight. So again we had second thoughts about this devise which could attract the attention of German aircraft, not to mention the police.

8

Towards the Real Thing

The year 1943 started badly for us boys, although it went well for Britain, improved for Russia but went downhill for Italy. For Germany it marked the start of the necessity to wage total war by involving the entire economy and population in the war effort to try to avoid losing against the three allies – Britain, Russia and America, with the latter proving to be the ally that Britain so needed and deserved. In the Pacific, by 1945, Japan faced a catastrophic experience, which the atomic age would make possible.

However, the war would unfold for another two and a half years and so we twins had the long-awaited opportunity to get 'into the act' and John Bray, Barry Earps, Alan and I were ready. We had made a solid start with our abortive early-warning contraption although it played no part in the Allied victory! This device had been installed on the roof of *The Limes* just as General Eisenhower took control of Allied forces in the United Kingdom. This symbolic coincidence appeared to have no real significance, or did it? In the interval between our decision to join the Army Cadets and the disbanding of our boys' unit, the hard-core members of the unit made it plain that they wanted to soldier on and a number of parents approached us to say how much they welcomed the participation of their son in our self-created unit. It gave their children a sense of purpose and an element of discipline that they all sadly lacked now that the schools were functioning well below par. One mother told Alan that our unit was the best thing next to a boys' club and much better than the Scouts. We also received much praise from parents for our weekly newsletter, written in pencil, which reported events in the neighbourhood not fully covered in the local newspaper. We often wrote about local bomb incidents in much greater detail because the local paper was subject to the censorship laws and we also included some real war news from the front as interpreted by me. Each copy of our weekly newsletter was written by me and then printed by hand but, unfortunately, we didn't keep any back copies as every edition of about twenty copies sold out on the day of publication, a Saturday. We charged one farthing

John Bray, ACF, 1943.

per copy and our readers said that each edition was worth more than the paper it was written on.

We still used our main headquarters at *The Limes* for early detection of possible air raids and when we detected incoming aircraft we passed a message to other strategically placed boys who would then blow whistles. This was not very successful so we tried to assemble a better version of our early detection device. Our new device was quite large since we were able to stretch a bamboo hoop found on a bomb site to 16 feet, which gave a larger circumference, the better to catch incoming sounds and to amplify them. This hoop was, like our earlier device, attached to surplus bed sheets and underpinned by stretched wallpaper which was painted white and then moulded into a bowl-like shape producing a smooth and flexible surface that was strong enough to withstand wind and rain. It looked like a gigantic ear. Sadly we failed to erect it before 20 January 1943 when the pilot of a Folke Wolf 19 fighter bomber swept over looking for targets and deliberately dropped a bomb on a school in Sandhurst Road, Catford. During the lunchtime school break the plane circled overhead flying at roof-top height and then the pilot waved to the children before dropping his bomb on the school killing forty four civilians, mostly children, and injuring sixty other people. We had seen the plane earlier as it roared overhead flying low as we went home to lunch on that dreadful day and we saw the pilot before his attack and he had seen us as we entered Mayday Gardens. He appeared to wave at us as we fell flat to the ground with our fingers held tightly in our ears. We instantly recognised it as a German fighter bomber and yet no air-raid warning sounded and there were no other German aircraft were in the vicinity.

His flight path was suicidally low and his manoeuvres were pursued aggressively in a manic search for a target.

He appeared to be either unhinged or totally indifferent to his own safety. All of his victims had been singled out by a pilot who must have known he was bombing a school in a densely populated area.

Later, when we read in the press and heard on the BBC news of the RAF's mass bombing of German cities, including the 1,000-bomber raids, we felt no pity for the Germans at all. Our whole family approved of the 'area bombing' by the RAF since we had gathered from a pilot on leave, who lived next door, that so called 'precision bombing' was a relative failure. We discussed this with our parents and teachers, all of whom showed a desire to hit back somehow or another at the Germans. Our local vicar, however, who later entertained German and Italian POWs at his vicarage, was outspoken in his criticism of strategic bombing on moral grounds. His parishioners did not agree and his vicarage lost several windows in isolated attacks by local youths.

In the early spring of 1943 we prepared ourselves for the Army Cadet Force but first had to persuade them that we were old enough to join. This was a bit difficult as we were still in short trousers, wore school blazers, were small for our age and did not look like teenagers. But Alan and I hit upon a ruse: we would borrow a pair of long trousers from Dad's wardrobe and attempt to join the Cadets along with John Bray and Barry Earps, both of whom were much taller and obviously more eligible. We chose to join one evening at the end of a humid day and this, combined with the first experience of wearing long, thick, winter trousers, gave us a red-faced almost Chaplinesque appearance. When I was asked my age by the Cadet under-officer I confessed that I was not fourteen yet. The under-officer, a lad of seventeen years, was very smart in his immaculate battledress. He wore a light khaki shirt with a webbing belt round his waist and his trousers were ironed to perfection, which instantly made our make-shift clothes look shabby beyond belief so he hesitated before enrolling us. Alan piped up to say that we were still at school and that due to the clothes rationing our parents had yet to replace our school uniforms so we had borrowed our father's trousers. He laughed and told us to line up behind the uniformed Cadets, well to the rear, with other ill-assorted boys seeking to join. We were in or would be once we had proved how serious we were by reporting to the battalion twice a week to undertake drill practice and other duties and so, after nearly two months of provisional membership, we were ordered to get our kit from the quartermaster's store. This was the most exciting experience of our lives so far and going home on the tram from Beresford Square we proudly carried our uniforms, which before we could actually wear them, were to require a lot of alterations. Our prize possession was a forage cap displaying the badge of the Royal West Kent Regiment. The victory at El Alamein the previous year had led General Montgomery to decree that ordinary soldiers could wear an open-necked battle dress blouse with a tie and shirt and so we adopted this new fashion with relish when we went on parade twice a week, learning to march with precision. The older boys looked like genuine soldiers; Alan and I looked like mascots.

We were now wearing the uniform that the soldiers who had died in the war had been wearing and we were proud to be associated with them. We began to read more about military operations, not least about the two Commando raids the previous year, on Saint Nazaire and the bigger attack on Dieppe. This was led by the 2nd Canadian Division and the British Commandos and consisted of a force of nearly six thousand. We had a personal interest in this raid, the tragic failure of which cost so many lives and could have included our father, as I explained earlier.

Back home in the garden Alan and I tried to restage these two operations on our hard-board battleground sited on top of the Anderson shelter, to which we added a water line to simulate the Channel coast and the sea off Dieppe. The St Nazaire raid had been a desperate business that brought limited success but excited us as a foretaste of things to come. Dieppe was regarded as a precursor of the eventual liberation of France and, though it was meticulously planned, it did not go well. The Canadians, who had never been in action before, faced formidable defences and were simply mown down by the German defenders and even when a reserve battalion was thrown into battle, it too was annihilated. The BBC was pretty honest about this, despite the censorship, and the raid did nothing to reassure us that the liberation of France was going to be easy.

My father informed Alan that Lord Louis Mountbatten, the overall commander of the operation, was over-promoted and had proved to be a lightweight figure playing the part of a heavyweight strategist. The poor Canadians had paid the price of his derring-doing and had suffered casualties in excess of 3,600 out of a raiding force twice that size. Nothing of value was learnt except, as Dad said, that we were incapable of seizing a working port without incurring appalling casualties. In his firm opinion the staff at Combined Operations therefore needed to rethink how best to conduct a successful amphibious operation. Mr Churchill, in overstating the tonic effect of the resounding victory at El Alamein, had, quite rightly, used this to raise the nation's spirits but we were depressed by the disaster at Dieppe although it was only a raid and not a major battle.

However, our morale had been raised by the 8th Army and its earlier successes in 1942, and by our war-gaming in the garden where the Germans were once again being defeated by the British Army. Our Army Cadet experience just got better and better when we attended a weekend camp at Aldershot with the Grenadier Guards, where they taught us to strip a Bren gun and how to undertake hand-to-hand fighting along the hedgerows and fields of a supposed battle. Our sergeant instructor congratulated Alan and me on not being spotted as we moved along the hedgerows although this possibly had more to do with our size than our clever concealment. We carried .303 rifles armed with blanks but, unknown to Captain Strand, the company's commanding officer, we had also collected several rounds of live ammunition which we stockpiled in our secret hideout beneath the floorboards of *The Limes* on Shooters Hill.

We twins were instrumental in arranging a mock attack on the local Home Guard by arrangement. Now active in the ACF we were successful in persuading our commanding officer that three platoons of cadets should take part in a training exercise to test the battle-worthiness of the Home Guards' position on the top of Shooters Hill, covering the famous golf course. It was jointly agreed that we would attack them at twelve noon on Saturday 25 September 1943 in a bid to approach their position without being observed. The Home Guard accepted this challenge knowing that their field of fire – blanks of course – gave the defenders an uninterrupted view of the approaching enemy forces. The cadets led by Sergeant-Major Waterhouse then proceeded to take the hill unopposed at 11 a.m. where we hid in the thick undergrowth, awaiting the arrival of the Home Guard at twelve noon. They turned up somewhat reluctantly and totally unaware of our presence. One of them was heard to say, 'Why are we bothering to play with these silly little boys?' The answer came swiftly and decisively when we rose to our feet and killed them all. Surprise in warfare always guaranteed success. They took their defeat in good humour and admitted that we'd out-thought them – and then they all de-camped to the local pub. The Home Guard did not stand a chance against cadets who were well trained to practice deception and knew how to hide themselves.

Over Sunday lunch a week later, we boys boasted to our parents about our defeat of the Home Guard through the use of stealth and guile. The ACF had put one over the old soldiers and middle-aged men of the Home Guard unit, supposedly defending their position at the top of Shooters Hill. Dad laughed at our description of how we occupied the Home Guard's HQ but told us that we had 'little to be proud of' since the tactical victory over them was more apparent than real. Dad pointed to a book lying on his shelf in the front room written by Captain Liddell-Hart called *The Defence of Britain*, which was published a few weeks before the outbreak of the war. In this book Liddell-Hart had argued that the growing strength of the defensive over the offensive could prevent a sudden breakthrough by German armoured divisions, if enough anti-tank defences were installed along an impregnable line. According to Dad he was dead wrong as German tanks had bypassed the French Maginot Line through the Ardennes forest in 1940, by violating the neutrality of Belgium, and eventually throwing the British into retreat. The lesson for France was that if you had a flawed overall strategy the tactics adopted didn't matter. What the Allies needed was a strategy of all out war which would require the invasion of France and the strategic bombing of Germany. Alan and I had no idea about the difference between tactics and strategy and were beginning to realise it was far more complicated than we thought.

We left Colfes Grammar School later in 1943, when all the combined schools regained their autonomy, to attend the Roan School where places had been reserved for us as our great-grandfather had, in 1880, been a prize-winning pupil. The school faced Greenwich Park near to Blackheath, where we had our first encounter with the headmaster, a certain taciturn Dr Gilbert, and his cane, for failing to complete our homework and for taking every Wednesday afternoon off, for our war work, rather than play soccer on the school's vast playing fields near Lee Green.

Our battlefront was now the home front where we fought on two flanks, our school and our parents, and although we lost both battles we won our personal war by sacrificing our future to our involvement in the war effort. Our capacity for self-laceration and self-deception proved a lethal cocktail, never to be resisted. The homework strike we organised at the Roan School was not supported by other boys and so Alan and I were completely isolated. We endured another painful caning and finally expulsion from the Roan School which we left in disgrace at the end of the autumn term. The Roan School period had, however, involved a dark secret, which neither we nor our parents ever openly revealed or discussed. It was one of those curious occurrences that defy explanation, but which can be seen as a metaphor for the 'boffin' culture of the war period. Our parents had insisted on a complete cover-up of the secret laboratory in the spare bedroom, which we had built up over several months. Its existence would have brought deep shame and disgrace for both us and for our long suffering parents because we had 'borrowed' all the equipment from school and had carried all this equipment back home in our school satchels after our weekly chemistry lessons.

The slow build-up of the secret lab had remained undetected by my mother since she had regarded the small bedroom upstairs as 'off-limits'. She had no idea that we had secreted an entire chemistry laboratory, including a Bunsen burner as well as a variety of chemicals. We were, optimistically, trying to make a secret bomb for use against Nazi Germany once we had made our breakthrough in scientific research, which was unlikely since we had absolutely no knowledge of chemistry or physics.

What inspired us to do this is a more interesting question but perhaps it was because we had read a book that my father had acquired. *Science and Life* written by Frederick Soddy, had been published in 1920 and it appeared that on 17 November 1915 Mr Soddy had told members of the Aberdeen Independent Labour Party about the possibility of a bomb utilising radio-active energy. Alan and I read the book from cover to cover in the autumn of 1943. Alan made an endless stream of dismal predictions inspired by the book such as 'if we fooled with science it would kill us all'. He kept asking, 'Is science to be the master or the servant of man?' I thought that Alan had taken leave of his senses, while John Bray pressed us to push ahead with the development of our own bomb.

At this time the entire country was unaware of the Manhattan Project, one of the best-kept secrets of the war, and one which only a few people in the War Cabinet were aware of. That project was a success whereas our version was a total failure, although it had at least remained a secret for some time.

Much later we learnt of the two wartime agreements, the Quebec Agreement of 1943 and the Hyde Park Agreement of September 1944, which set up the Anglo-American atomic project. British, Canadian, and American scientists combined together in a bid to produce an atomic bomb in quick order before a German or Japanese breakthrough occurred. There was a desperate need to be the first to produce a fissionable bomb which indeed occurred in 1944. All this took place in the USA at the Los Alamos laboratory in New Mexico where a brilliant team of physicists created a device of unprecedented destructive power initially with the intent for use against Germany. However, by the time of its successful first test in April 1945 Germany was on the verge of surrender and President Roosevelt was dead.

After our unsuccessful effort to develop a bomb we decided to organise a funfair on the green in Mayday Gardens, which was, in the event, attended by more than fifty people and was the most successful local community event since King George VI's coronation in 1936. The purpose of the funfair was to raise money for 'Spitfire Week' and we eventually raised £50. Helped by a school friend's father who was a company director, we managed to borrow a large marquee, several tents, and a loudspeaker from Johnson and Philips, a local factory producing radio equipment, which the company kept for its annual sports day. We also opened our own local theatre in John Bray's father's capacious shed, which we called the 'Kit-Kat' Theatre. Plays were enacted by us, all on themes to do with love, death and war, although our seating capacity was actually smaller than the number of performers on stage. We made a modest charge for these productions, which went towards the costs of production and paying our out-of-pocket expenses.

But our theatre was nearly, quite literally, undermined when John Bray inexplicably started digging for coal in his back garden and excavated a huge hole under the shed. His deep shaft alarmed us, and his near neighbours, and John was forced to abandon his search for coal so we turned our attention to building a submarine with the intention of submerging it in the local fire service emergency water tank, which now occupied the site of the bombed out houses in Mayday Gardens. As the submarine was neither waterproof nor buoyant, Harry Savage nearly drowned during the launch of this floating coffin. His life was only saved by the heroic efforts of Alan and a new boy now living nearby, Joseph Aspell, whose Irish family were renting a house at the top end of the road. Joseph was a little bit older than we were and was a welcome addition to our group. We were in good spirits as the year 1943 drew to a close.

9

From the Little Blitz to D-Day

From our personal perspective the pace of the war now appeared to accelerate bringing new opportunities as well as some nasty shocks. In early 1944 we left the Army Cadets Force [ACF] to join the Air Cadets [ATC]. Why? Well we had achieved our objectives in the ACF by learning something about land warfare, but in reality we were not yet old enough to get the promotion we thought we deserved in the ACF, despite creating a favourable impression with our commanding officer, Captain Strand. We were also a bit frustrated that Cadet Sergeant Ted Waterhouse, who we liked, had just been promoted to Sergeant-Major and therefore showed no signs of wanting to leave so, for the time being, we thought we would try our luck with the Air Cadets as we had heard that they were looking for a couple of musicians for their band and we fancied becoming drummers despite having no obvious talent or skills.

We really didn't have much of an ear for music, although we did like the romantic music that came to Britain with the arrival of the American Army. We liked popular songs such as 'Love Letters' performed by the English vocalist Dick Haynes. We admired the singing of Anne Shelton and Marlene Dietrich, particularly the latter's rendition of the song 'Lilly Marlene', a melody first heard on German radio. We liked Diana Shaw and Dorothy Careless, both of whom were very popular especially with the British forces exuding, as they did, both femininity and sex appeal.

We found the ATC very different from the ACF in ways that were both pleasing and off-putting. Our squadron HQ was in a large, requisitioned Victorian house close to Lee Green and was on the tram route to Lewisham. Instead of the army battledress we now wore the blue uniform of the ATC, which buttoned up to the neck with bright silver buttons. This actually had the effect of making us look younger than we had in Army battledress and so was rather unfortunate as we were still small for our age.

We took our place in the band but our musical talents, or lack thereof, well established by Alan in the earlier episode of the piano and Jean Stoddart, quickly resulted in our relegation to marching with the band without musical instruments during ceremonial events. But our lack of success in yet another thing did not dismay us.

The band rehearsed in Vanbrugh Castle, a rather splendid pseudo-castle, positioned at the top of Maze Hill, Greenwich, but which was disquietingly close to the Roan School from which we had been expelled. We actually bumped into our former headmaster, Dr Gilbert, whom we acknowledged politely. He had clearly pretended not to know us since he smiled in the distant way of a man who had no idea who we were. Actually he did know who we were, he just preferred to forget us. Ten years later Alan became a governor of the school as he was a local councillor in the mid-1950s and Alan's re-appearance improved his memory.

As members of the ATC we were expected to attend maths classes twice a week at a school in Plumstead from which we derived some marginal benefit. The incentive for all cadets to do so was to eventually qualify for air crew, which meant that air cadets were overall better educated than our contemporaries in the ACF. The ATC was distinctly more middle-class than the ACF and, in fact, many of the Cadets did end up as pilots, navigators, radio engineers, and even rear gunners. Although these maths lessons were rather like being back at school, they were a great deal more focused on the war and this pleased us. What we could not have known at the time was how the ATC would give us a bird's eye view of the cross channel invasion now imminent.

The second front, which everyone was now anxious to see get under away had long preoccupied our thoughts. Gwen, who had by now returned to London, was an Essex County Council supply teacher and so more or less took over our education. One evening she got the family to play a new game based on sliding an upturned glass across the surface of a mirror laid flat on a table. We weren't allowed to push the glass but we could rest our hands on it as it slid across the mirror's surface. On the outer circumference of the mirror we stuck tiny pieces of paper displaying the dates on which the liberation of Europe might possibly commence. To our subsequent astonishment Gwen's glass slid towards 5 June, which proved to be the actual date for the invasion, which was, in the event, postponed by one day due to bad weather.

Dad's work on the Thames gave him a bird's eye view of the logistical back-up for the invasion that was well underway by early spring 1944. He told us about some strange objects and odd-looking blocks of concrete stowed in barges and ships and being taken down the Thames towards the entrance of the Medway River. We boys decided to cycle to Chatham to see what was going on in what was a prohibited area. We always took light camping kit with us, just in case an over-night stay was necessary due to enemy action. This included a small blanket each and a tiny amount of food, as well as some heavy clothing in case of bad weather. We saw some extraordinary things. Dad was right. There were bits and pieces of concrete or whatever being assembled, presumably for the invasion. We saw much evidence of military mayhem and confusion being created. We decided to penetrate the prohibited area on our bikes and discovered a huge phantom fleet of landing craft surrounded by fields packed with wood and canvas tanks with an assortment of other vehicles surrounded by long lines of empty marquees and tents. We spent the night in one of these tents beside a large dummy aircraft parked in a dispersal pen on a pretend airfield. The illusion was created that the Allies had a vast army stationed in Kent, but as far as we could see, there wasn't a soldier in sight. Using our acquired field-craft skills to get into and out of this vast base, we managed to sit on an inflatable rubber Sherman tank before being chased off at gun-point by an American soldier. The allied plan, therefore, presumably seemed to be to trick the Germans into thinking the landing would take place between the Rhine and Pas-de-Calais area. We knew nothing about the deception plan but we guessed it was part of an Allied strategy to fool the Nazi war machine into thinking that the invasion was imminent. It did occur to us that maybe we weren't going to invade Europe at all and that we'd got cold feet. We discovered the truth of what was going on sometime later when the Air Ministry sent us to an ATC camp in the West Country. Actually, we ended up with the Fleet Air Arm being trained by the Royal Navy.

We arrived, however, somewhat surprisingly, at the Royal Naval Fleet Air Arm station at Henstrich in Somerset over the weekend of the 2/3 June 1944, just prior to the invasion, and found ourselves confined to our 'ship', as the Navy called all shore establishments, for the next week or so. We were surrounded by British, Canadian, and Polish troops and the US 29th Division, and so we were about to witness one of the greatest events in modern history.

We were told that we were to live under canvas alongside deep trenches dug for our protection against any possible German retaliatory attacks once the invasion had commenced. We were issued with military-type gas masks and steel helmets and we were told that we were under military discipline and that if we tried to leave the ship we could be shot! Nonetheless, we managed to talk to some of the soldiers, over a barbed wire fence, who told us that the invasion would take place within the next couple of days despite it having been delayed because of the miserable weather. The idea that nobody knew that the invasion was imminent made the secrecy surrounding 'Operation Overlord' something of a myth. We were all very excited by the prospect of invasion and, indeed, on the Monday evening we heard the roar of hundreds upon hundreds of bombers flying out to sea to attack targets in France to soften up the German defences before our troops went in. It was clear to us that southern England had become a vast armed camp. A Polish officer told Alan that an enormous armada had been assembled and was ready to sail and that he had seen hundreds of thousands of troops moving to embarkation ports as part of 'Operation Overlord'. Obviously total secrecy was only relative in nature given the rapid spread of well-informed rumours.

After our encounter with the soldiers but before the start of the invasion, we witnessed an attack on cadet Barry Earps. Barry was stretched out naked on a table surrounded by yelling cadets as senior boys brushed his genitals with stinging nettles. As he was screaming with pain some of the cadets tried to go to his rescue to bring this ugly scene to a close and indeed both Alan and I were threatened with similar treatment for our efforts to help Barry. Too small to fight for Barry's dignity we protested loudly to a cadet NCO, who simply laughed and turned his gaze away as the torment continued. What was behind this ugly attack on this quite harmless boy we'd known since his sixth birthday? Was it just a boys' prank or had he done something to provoke it? The answer was never forthcoming except that Barry was one of life's victims. He was tall for his age and rather good looking but had slightly protruding teeth. This together with his blonde hair gave Barry a slightly effete appearance but he was neither effeminate in demeanour nor in his speech or posture. In fact, his interest in the opposite sex was only exceeded by mine. Seeing him attacked in this way on the eve of the greatest day in our lives gave us pause for thought and Barry later confessed to hoping that a German air attack would kill his tormentors.

It had been Barry who had encouraged us to join the Air Cadets, because he thought there would be the chance of a flight in an aircraft as well as the opportunity to put to good use our skills in aircraft recognition which air cadets were expected to have. To see Barry put through this great indignity by older boys was simply appalling so we decided to take action. We quickly organised a posse of older cadets to provide him with a bodyguard for the remainder of his stay at Henstrich which ensured that the incident was never repeated. We had deterred any further assaults by acting together in self-defence – or was it really collective defence?

In the late evening of Monday 5 June 1944 the 'ship's' commander addressed the entire crew on the tannoy and announced that the liberation of Europe would begin at dawn and that we must all expect a German attack on the airfield. All cadets were ordered to spend the night in the trenches, covered by blankets, and told to keep our gas masks and tin hats close to hand. Any attempt to leave the 'ship' would be treated as a serious breach of naval discipline since the success of the invasion depended on total secrecy.

His voice rang out with just the hint of a tremor, which conveyed both supreme urgency and barely suppressed excitement. We all jumped up and down and cheered feeling that our day had come. We felt that we stood together with the entire nation and that, in a deeper if remote way, we were part of the armada that would set sail for the French coast. What a moment! We had little sleep that night as the bombers passed overhead and we waited for dawn to break. Would the invasion be successful? Our initial excitement gave way to a growing anxiety about it all. We weren't allowed to phone home so, inevitably, we felt isolated and alone despite being surrounded by about seventy cadets about to experience an event of biblical proportions. Little did we realise what would unfold just six days after the Allied troops had fought their way ashore on the Normandy beaches and which would propel Alan and myself into a different sort of battle – but more of that later. D-Day itself, however, fulfilled all our heightened expectations given that the initial radio reports were so optimistic and so we gained no impression of the slaughter on Omaha Beach, which the Americans experienced in the early days of the invasion.

We were told by our NCOs on D-Day plus four that we had now been given permission to resume normal training, which was to include a flight in a trainer aircraft as soon as the weather conditions improved and so within a couple of days we were actually airborne – if only briefly! We would see with our own eyes the extraordinary array of ships, both large and small, all moving in one direction – towards France. They were like dots on the grey, choppy sea. Our Polish pilot had given other cadets a bad time with his loop-the-loops, which had resulted in a lot of vomiting and screaming. Alan and I somewhat timorously climbed into the aircraft and, because we were relatively small, we were allowed to go together in the same plane. The pilot had a hard and resolute face; he wanted to be fighting the Germans rather than joy riding a bunch of teenagers over the fields of Somerset and Devon. He appeared though to take pity on us and asked us whether we were really fourteen so we owned up to the fact that we weren't actually fourteen until the end of November. He then asked us in a very gentle voice what we wanted to see. 'Well sir,' I said, 'we have never flown in an aircraft before only in a glider but we'd love to see something of the invasion' and this seemed to please him. 'Let's see what we can do,' he said. The plane roared down the runway for takeoff and then the buildings below gradually began to shrink. How small the ships and barrage balloons below seemed as we veered towards the coastline. The noise of the engine increased as he banked towards the line of ships stretched out below as far as the eye could see. Our pilot, whose name we could never pronounce or remember, indicated that he thought he had enough fuel to reach the landing beaches and possibly get back. The plane did several rather violent manoeuvres and then, at an alarmingly low altitude, was soon skimming over the ships in the vast expanse of the English Channel and, as the English coast started to recede, we were now completely confused as to where we were and where we were heading. What if we crashed in France and had fallen into the hands of the Germans? Would they have regarded us as prisoners of war?

Our pilot was certainly living up to the reputation of the Poles for derring-do so could it actually be the D-Day beaches below us? Surely not as it was in fact Southampton. But we were convinced that it was Cherbourg and that we were over France as we witnessed the endless detritus of war on a scale we never could have imagined. What we were seeing, in reality, was the long lines of ships to the south of the Isle of Wight. We landed safely back on terra firma with such a buzz of excitement that it overwhelmed both our common sense and our rather limited grasp of geography. Our Polish pilot begged us not to tell anyone that we'd been over to Normandy as he would face a court martial for his pains but we could not keep the secret for long. During the following weeks we told everyone of our flight over Normandy and so successful were we in recounting this story that eventually the editor of the local newspaper, *Kentish Mercury,* contacted us to arrange an interview about the story. Gwen had innocently told a school friend, whose father was the editor of the newspaper, of her twin brothers' flight over France after the D-Day landings. The newspaper, who sent their top reporter to interview us, quickly concluded that the Polish pilot had hoodwinked us and so the Williams twins were denied their moment of glory. Yet we retold this greatly embellished story for years to come and still half-believe that it actually happened. Who knows?

The reality was less dramatic; we were both sent to work in the galley helping the Wrens prepare food for the crew of the ship. The Wrens were amused by our response to the BBC news relayed on the tannoy as we stood rigidly to attention to hear every word. Both of us regarded ourselves as on active service though our work was far from dangerous or exacting. Most of the other cadets were engaged in activities that we were judged to be incapable of performing although we saw things very differently; like the Wrens we were doing war work.

Once back home again in Mayday Gardens we were brought quickly down to earth by hearing, in the small hours of 12 June 1944, a most unusual noise overhead as a huge bombing onslaught hit London. We'd never seen such strange-looking aircraft that belched flames and caused such a hideous noise but, misguidedly, we cheered as we assumed that the Ack-Ack guns on Woolwich Common had hit an incoming German bomber. Then shortly afterwards another aircraft came into view, which, again, appeared to have been hit by the defending AA guns as it flew noisily over Broad Walk. We did notice, however, that the flak had not caused the aircraft to change course and it was soon lost to view. Seconds later we heard a loud bang in the near distance. What on earth was going on? This was in fact the start of Hitler's secret weapons attack on the people of southern England and of London in particular. Local people now took to the shelters and children were once again to be evacuated and so we reluctantly left for Nottingham, with our mother, for the summer while our father remained behind. The so-called 'Terror' weapons had arrived with a vengeance and were soon to be popularly known as 'Doodlebugs' or 'Buzz Bombs' as they descended on London in great and hideous profusion. We left for Nottingham on 7 July 1944 with thousands of other children but, as ever, we were determined to get back to London as soon as possible. This was no time to quit the battle.

10

The Nottingham Interlude

We enjoyed living in Nottingham for the few brief weeks we were there. It was a nice interlude during which we enjoyed life in this city in almost ideal circumstances. We were housed in a working-class area in a back-to-back terrace house which was sparsely furnished with no bathroom, so we had to go to the municipal baths provided for the neighbourhood. Mum did our cooking and ironing while Alan and I did our flirting. To our immense surprise we were much sought after by the pretty girls of Nottingham – and how pretty they were and how available for escapist romantic love. The girls were intrigued by our accents and our self-confident attitude. The teenage girls were dressed to attract and our hormones were on the rise, so we took to the rather curvaceous adolescent girls like ducks to water. To Mum's surprise we were no longer quite so interested in the war. To caress a young girl's breast was found to be greatly more pleasurable than clutching a Lee Enfield rifle as we had in the Army Cadets, or collecting shrapnel.

Perhaps our heightened sensual feelings helped to make Nottingham so memorable for both of us. It had a lot to do with us growing as well as the after effects of the bromide, which allegedly had been put into our tea during the unforgettable stay at Henstrich.

Alan said to me that the bromide was put in the tea to ward off sexual feelings for the Wrens at the Fleet Air Arm station as the men outnumbered the women. Now that our tea was unadulterated our sexual feelings had risen fairly sharply.

By the time we reached Nottingham we had become quite anti-German, though for different reasons. We hardly bothered to make the distinction between the Nazis and other Germans and Nottingham was far away from either group as we settled in to our new abode. A strong sense of escapism contrasted with our previous determination to get into the war. Yet events were now moving fast; on 20 July 1944 Hitler was nearly killed by a bomb left in his Wolf's Lair in East Prussia and just five days earlier Field Marshall Rommel was seriously hurt when his car was attacked by Allied fighters. We boys felt that we were now in the wrong place. These dramatic events required us to be in London, not over 130 miles away in Nottingham. Yet Hitler's onslaught on London continued unabated while we had escaped to a bomb-free Nottingham in indecent haste.

The initial reception at Nottingham Midland Railway station was friendly and efficient. We unloaded our bags and were escorted to a bus awaiting the arrival of evacuees from London. The bus took us through the centre of Nottingham, known as the lace market, up and on to the road leading to the back-to-back Victorian houses situated high above the town, yet within walking distance of the impressive public buildings which overlooked the main square below. As the bus slowly climbed the sharp hill behind the town hall, with factories on both sides of the road, it became obvious that we were to live in the old houses built for the skilled workers in the small local factories. This was the business and industrial heart of the thriving city that had survived the worst effects of the 1930s recession. We were interested in the factories that produced a wide range of goods and services. John Player began his tobacco business here, Raleigh bicycles were manufactured, and Jessie Boots created the nationwide chemist chain. His shops had a bookish feel about them with their inexpensive lending library and their antiseptic pharmaceuticals sold by assistants in white coats. This unique combination of medical products and penny-a-week book-lending suggested to us a strong protestant work ethic confirmed by the solid buildings and the sturdy appearance of the local people. In the densely populated neighbourhood, with its cobbled roads and poorly lit streets, the women were relatively well dressed and seemed less anxious than their London counterparts. It was high summer, which gave the neighbourhood a light, if intimate, appearance and the cheek-by-jowl shops and churches generated a genuine community atmosphere. There were few trees in the neighbourhood, although beyond the suburban streets lay green fields stretching into the distance. We were housed with a friendly family, whose well-kept house reminded us of the better seaside guest houses of the period. This might not be Clacton-on-Sea but it was wholesome and secure and there were no doodlebugs here – but no bathrooms either.

These Nottingham people had opened their homes to evacuees having had little warning of the mass arrivals of evacuees from south-east London, who were as diverse as the neighbourhoods in London had always been. A Mrs Green and her son from Kidbrooke, who was about our age and who shared our interests in a rather priggish way, were housed in the same street. Mrs Green was very superior and worshipped regularly at the local Catholic cathedral. Alan and I were nominally Church of England but were largely ignorant of the rituals of Christian worship. Richard Green was a studious boy who had been at a good school near Blackheath and he was astonished to hear of our exploits.

At that time I was looking slightly emaciated as just before we left for Nottingham we had cycled to Brighton and back, losing over a stone in weight. Alan was riding a very big bike, much too big for him, but he lost much less weight since he was already more solid-looking than me and was also more cheerful and sociable. As a result Mrs Green regarded me with some dubiety, and not a little anxiety, given the number of girls waiting outside the house as she attributed my rather shrunken appearance to sexual activity rather than to my exertion on my bike. Yet Alan was actually the great girl-chaser, and he hid this side of his character rather better than I could manage. Mrs Green once said to my mother that I appeared less gregarious than my twin brother Alan, to which Mum replied that I was the introvert and Alan the extrovert. Alan was the future politician and much dined 'man about town' while I was to become the academic.

I do not wish to paint a bad picture of our morals, since we both shared a modest and realistic approach to teenage sexual activity. We knew how far to go in a social climate then far less liberal than the 1960s and beyond. On a scale of one to ten we rarely got above five, but we lived during a period when sexual mores were changing rapidly given the sudden departure of husbands and boyfriends to the war and the mass arrival of young soldiers and airmen from America. As far as we could judge most women and young girls had American boyfriends, which on occasion could result in fisticuffs when their husbands or boyfriends returned home on leave.

The Americans were really enforced tourists whose arrival in Britain had had a sensational impact on British society. By summer 1944 most of the Americans in Britain were airmen, since the majority of their soldiers were in France post-D-Day, but it was rare to see an American without a woman in tow. The Americans obviously enjoyed an English pint of beer and waited patiently in the queues to go to the pictures. During our stay we also visited a rather posher area, south of the town centre and just over Trent Bridge, called West Bridgford. There, in a Victorian villa, we met a senior American officer who was serving in the US Army Air Corps. He said to me that his greatest anxiety about his stay in Britain related to his men and how they behaved; sex and racial problems had been his biggest headaches ever since he arrived in Britain in January 1942. 'British women,' he said, 'had been transformed by the war itself and a surprising number surrendered themselves to the Americans who were better paid and dressed than their English boyfriends or husbands.' Alan and I thought that the problem of the American forces being 'over paid, oversexed and over here' was indeed very real, since so many of them wanted to marry English girls and apparently some 30,000 had already done so! Perhaps, however, the trickiest problem was segregation in the American forces now living in a British society unused to racial segregation and racial discord.

But what was life like for the average serving American before the D-Day landings? Presumably the soldiers were well trained since their personal survival rate would depend on their fitness as soldiers and not on their sexual athleticism, and indeed they were then being tested on the beaches of Normandy. There had been over a million US men hanging around in Britain before D-Day, in a state of great uncertainty and in some ignorance of what the war was about. We discovered this when we spoke to some of the less educated airmen and soldiers who said to us that they resented being here at all! Most looked younger than their British counterparts and hailed from the more remote and less sophisticated parts of the United States. In any event, we gathered that the number of illegitimate children in Britain had certainly increased by the time they had left for Normandy in June. But we liked the Americans' spontaneity and cheerfulness and they certainly demonstrated their bravery in battle.

By the end of the summer it was time to return to London, and we got back to Mayday Gardens in August 1944, by which time the V2 ballistic missiles were about to supersede the V1s or Doodlebugs in the strategic bombardment of London.

We were actually back at school in early September when on the 8th, without any warning, there was a shattering explosion caused by the world's first ballistic missile – the V2. We immediately volunteered to serve as messengers in the National Fire Service [NFS] just a matter of weeks before our fourteenth birthday and managed to persuade the NFS that we were old enough to enrol. We were fitted out with a blue uniform, an NFS cap and badge, a steel helmet, a proper gas mask, and a greatcoat. Now at long last we were to play a real part in the defence of London.

We returned to London to resume our war with two of our favourite jokes about Americans. One GI said to another, 'We gotta, gotta see Coventry. They tell me a naked woman rides through the streets on a horse.' His buddy replied, 'Yeah, let's go I ain't seen a horse for years.' This joke was capped by a more explicit comment that a new brand of knickers were on the market – 'One yank and they're off.' When we told these jokes to John Bray he said that when we had won the war Jane, of the *Daily Mirror*, the heroine of the daily strip cartoon, would appear completely naked for the first time. Now the entire nation looked forward to victory!

Above left: Alan Lee Williams, NFS, 1944.

Above right: Geoffrey Lee Williams, NFS, 1944.

11

The National Fire Service

We joined the National Fire Service as part-time messengers with almost no really serious training, although we already had plenty of experience of riding a bike. The fire station was in Plumstead High Street, which backed onto the Woolwich Arsenal and our responsibilities were to maintain communications between headquarters and the fire engines attending an incident, as well as making ourselves available for other duties as directed by a senior officer. We were now on duty in an official capacity for the first time since 3 September 1939. The experience was to prove testing yet memorable, at times exciting, but frightening.

At the beginning of September all was confusion. Did the V2 exist or not? The government denied the existence of the V2s and said that the increasing number of unexplained 'gas mains' exploding was merely accidental. John Bray, who had also joined the NFS with us, thought otherwise: 'It's a new weapon,' he declared, with all the confidence of the son of a Regimental Sergeant Major, and we could find no-one at the Fire Station who disagreed with him. However, within weeks the government confirmed that Hitler's Germany did have a new terror weapon and we were able to confirm this for ourselves after we attended an incident on the fringe of Castle Wood in early October 1944. In fact it turned out to be part of a rocket that had disintegrated in flight in the sky above central Woolwich. This was not known to us until after the war.

John Bray, NFS,
1944.

We still have a very clear recollection of the incident. We
arrived at the scene some twenty minutes after the event.
The V2 had struck some trees on the steep incline beneath
the castle, causing some slight damage to the houses below
and setting fire to trees and shrubbery. It wasn't a big fire
but nonetheless we reported to the Senior Fire Officer
attending the incident, as all such bombings were called.
His attention was focused, however, on the fire which was
spreading further into the woods and towards the castle. He
told us to go home since we had not been officially called
to the bomb site by 'Control' and appeared indifferent to

our presence, but we decided to stay on to be of help with the investigation of the cause of the explosion. The police, the ARP, and the firemen were now deployed over an area of about 2,000 yards searching for evidence and quelling the small fires crackling away in the dry undergrowth, but no-one found anything like an exposed gas pipe or even smelt gas, although we did uncover some old piping and I found a Roman coin in remarkably good condition. This was definitely not a gas main explosion. Yet the government still insisted on the gas main cover story. It was apparent to all that the earlier doodlebugs, which had killed some 6,000 civilians and injured possibly three times as many, had now been replaced by a new terror weapon against which there was no means of defence. It was all the more unnerving because it seemed so unreal. No air-raid sirens sounded and not even the noise of an approaching aircraft was heard. Nothing at all until the sound of the explosion itself by which time, of course, people were either dead or were aware of the ghastly sound of rushing air, like that of a screaming banshee, sucking the life out of the atmosphere. The war of the cities had taken a sinister turn.

We assumed that the official NFS report of this incident must have contradicted the official explanation because by 10 November 1944 the government admitted that it was a V2, a ballistic rocket, the first of its kind. Between September 1944 and March 1945 we subsequently attended about eight such incidents in the Woolwich and Greenwich boroughs, all of which involved V2 rockets as well as roughly six earlier incidents involving V1s. We were volunteers but did get our travelling expenses paid, a modest sum amounting to rather less than a pound a month. All of our 'turn outs' for the NFS followed a similar pattern although during the worst incident I was with a local girl at the cinema that evening. Alan therefore 'turned out' without me and the incident was to prove his greatest hour and his worst experience. As such it is worth recalling in some detail.

The carnage at the Brook Hotel, a pub on Shooters Hill outside the entrance to the Brook Hospital, occurred at 6.40 p.m. on 11 November 1944, coincidentally Armistice Day. The V2 rocket struck the pub and a number 89 London Transport bus, which had stopped to pick up passengers outside. There was standing room only on this bus so within seconds most of these passengers were incinerated as well as some of the customers at the pub who were either killed outright or severely injured. In all over eighty people were killed and an unknown number injured, most of whom required medical treatment. The Brook Hospital, right next door, was almost overwhelmed by the dead and dying.

The nearby Woolwich Barracks ordered soldiers to go to help at this desperate scene. People had died where they were sitting on the bus or in the pub and the dreadful sweet smell of burning flesh, the rancid smell of burning timber and the thick dust pervaded the night air. Those in the pub who had survived stumbled out onto the road and dropped to the ground in shock, many of them hysterical.

Alan said that the less injured among them struggled to their feet to help others around them – the quick and the dead. The missile's warhead had, in one fatal, fleeting moment, struck the bus, slicing it in half and hurling the passengers into the air causing instantaneous dismemberment and death. Alan, sitting on a 72 tram just outside Shooters Hill police station, a short distance away, was one of the first on the scene and, dressed in his fire service uniform, was ready to help. No fire engine or ambulance had yet arrived, blocked as they were by the debris scattered along the old Roman road. Alan saw the bodies of people sitting on the upper deck of the bus, which had melted into strange shapes imitating life itself. It was so horrid that despite the sound of breaking glass and the crackling of flames he was only aware of an appalling silence. As he anticipated from his previous experiences passive crowds soon assembled transfixed by the carnage and overwhelmed by what they saw. Most people were mute, reduced to the role of spectators awaiting the arrival of the emergency services – the fire engines, the ambulances and the light and heavy rescue teams.

Alan tried to direct the crowd away from the stricken area to clear a way for the soldiers and rescuers to get to the debris of the Brook Hotel whose rooms were now exposed to the elements. The bus had largely disintegrated though the driver, dead in his cab, still clutched the steering wheel as if ready to drive away. The arrival of the NFS units and ambulances drawn from a wide area brought some sort of order to the chaos. As I sat on a tram crossing the intersection between the Well Hall Road and Shooters Hill, I knew something awful had occurred. A blinding flash had lit up the early evening sky and a huge explosion echoed around like a clap of thunder, but I decided to continue my journey to Beresford Square to meet my new girlfriend and to see an Abbot and Costello film at the Woolwich Gaumont.

Meanwhile my twin brother was otherwise engaged tearing away at the fallen bricks covering the injured and dying at the Brook Hotel. Above the noise of the fire pumps he heard someone screaming, which seemed to come from the back of the building away from the hectic rescue operations taking place. Alan climbed over the rubble and discovered the remnants of a bedroom with a teenage girl screaming in terror. Alan threw his NFS Great Coat over her and took her to one of the ambulances parked nearby. Little did Alan know who she was and, in his efforts to save her dignity, he looked away from her terrified face. She was in fact a neighbour, the daughter of Chief Inspector Chapman of the

Flying Squad who lived at the bottom of Mayday Gardens and was greatly feared by the local criminals and miscreants. A few days later when some of the facts about that night had emerged, Chief Inspector Chapman called at our house and told my mother that if her boys ever needed his protection or advice they could rely on Scotland Yard. Our astonished mother was shocked to hear that we might need police protection from our own follies but, as she already knew of Alan's heroic deed which had earned him much praise, she was somewhat critical of me for, rather typically I'm afraid, putting my social life first.

By the end of 1944 it was hoped that victory was at last in sight as people were exhausted and not a little demoralised by these attacks. Yet the news from the front soon darkened when, in the autumn, Montgomery's Operation Market Garden, with the battles at Arnhem and Nijmegen, produced disappointing results and heavy losses. But as Alan said to me, 'there's many a slip twixt cup and lip', quoting the only bit of Shakespeare he was familiar with, and indeed there was worse to come. On 16 December 1944, Hitler launched his counter offensive by smashing through the American lines in the Ardennes. We were baffled and shocked as we rushed to our battle board on top of the Anderson shelter to play out the brutal Panzer attacks, which had brought the Germans almost to Antwerp, the great Allied supply base. Our friends and neighbours had little to celebrate.

Things in the autumn of 1944 were changing on our domestic front too with the approach of our fourteenth birthday at the end of November; we had now legally left school. Alas Gwen's teaching efforts had come to an end when she went up to Lady Margaret Hall, Oxford, and plans were now afoot for us to be apprenticed to our father for seven years as Watermen and Lightermen, once we reached fourteen and a half years of age in 1945. Although seven years apprenticeship seemed an eternity to us our thoughts were still on the war which, after all, had lasted over five years already.

Alan and I were getting more and more political with Alan declaring himself to be a socialist and telling John Bray that the post-war recovery would call for the sort of planning that had come into existence during Churchill's war time coalition government. In personal terms freedom for us came on the day we left school and, as we walked home from school for the last time, a thick fog descended like a metaphor for the uncertainty we faced. We had burnt our boats in our determination to give the war absolute priority over our education and so now life without the war seemed an unreal situation for us even though we wanted it to end with an Allied victory.

It was a mixed picture for Alan and me since big personal challenges lay ahead. The war had a sting in its tail for us civilians. We will remember until our dying days the busy Saturday lunchtime, at the end of November just four days before our birthday, when a missile hit the rear of the Woolworths store in New Cross Road and the building collapsed in a cloud of dust, killing over 160 people. It was the worst V2 incident of the entire war. For the people of Lewisham the sky literally fell in. Alan and I cycled home to Blackheath deep in conversation about what we had seen. What if Hitler sent huge numbers of missiles with larger warheads carrying more destructive explosives? It was already clear to us that Germany was facing the destruction of its cities on a scale sufficient to force Germany to accept defeat. Would the same thing happen to Britain if German missiles had rained from the air in such numbers that they devastated London in like fashion? Then, in the early spring of 1945, we came face to face with death ourselves in what was to be one of the last V2 attacks of the war. We were saved by a low tide on the River Thames and by an incredible stroke of luck.

We enjoyed our final wartime Christmas with our parents producing a splendid, if scaled down, version of the festivities given the shortage of luxury items. We made pretty paper chains and decorations for the Christmas tree and for Christmas lunch we enjoyed roast chicken and vegetables followed by Christmas pudding made from whatever ingredients were available at the time.

12

A Lucky Escape

The shock effect of the German offensive before Christmas seemed to be an ominous warning: the war, both in Europe and the Far East, was not yet over. More shocks were likely and indeed followed in short order when we attended the Jackson Street incident on 17 March in Woolwich. The street had been struck by a V2 missile. It was not the degree of damage done to Jackson Street which, if anything, was not out of the ordinary with thirty-six houses destroyed and twice that number badly damaged. Some fifteen people were killed and at least one hundred injured, but it was the injuries sustained by the hapless residents that day that astonished us.

We arrived on our bikes shortly after the explosion, by which time the ambulances and fire appliances had circled the worst-affected houses. We reported to the NFS fire control unit for our orders, if any. There was little for us to do in terms of communication or control so initially we were told that we weren't required, but then a senior fire officer ordered us to identify and collect human remains. These were to be deposited in large dustbins supplied by the ARP light rescue who took responsibility for this gruesome task. Identification of the bodies, often without limbs or heads and lying around like abandoned meat, was a shocking experience but nonetheless Alan and I set about the systematic collection of the human remains. We had seen dead bodies before but had never seen human remains covered in blood and filth and lying on the pavement. It was horrible and nearly made us sick, yet we toiled away, searching for the remains of the dead, although Alan, who had experienced even worse scenes at the Brook Hospital, appeared less affected than John and I. The bins were full of bits and pieces of human anatomy, which included brains, legs and intestines. John picked up a human hand holding a spoon – that was one meal never to be enjoyed. We barely spoke about it afterwards and never told Mum and Dad about the events that day, which certainly testified that the final phase of the Battle of London was horrific. By this time the war had slipped into an ugly and brutal routine and to escape this we needed some sort of normality. This came when we joined the labour force as apprentice Watermen and Lightermen on the Thames on 13 March 1945. We were becoming young men rather than boys and so became rather more sensitive about some of the things that we had witnessed during the war.

Alan started going to local youth clubs calling for the Germans, including the general population and not just the political and military leadership, to be subject to a rigorous military occupation once victory was secured. He was most adamant that the surrender of Germany be absolute and unconditional. There could be no separate peace. His meetings provoked a great deal of interest and debate though he rarely spoke for more than ten minutes. Alan did, however, attract the attention of some influential Labour supporters who were to play a big part in preparing Alan for his future political life, which in due course started with his chairmanship of the Greenwich League of Youth.

Our interest was beginning to shift to the world of work, which had started before we took up our apprenticeship with the Union Lighterage Company in March 1945. I worked for Fisher's Military Tailors in Woolwich and Alan worked for Ragoul Levy, a local tailor who made suits and general clothing. We both received 20s a week for serving customers and making tea. Fisher's was a well-established manufacturer of uniforms for the armed services with a long pedigree of satisfying the needs of the nearby Royal Military Academy as well as supplying quality boots, shirts, and accessories for the officers of the NFS and the police. Mr Fisher employed his own tailor but also employed groups of Jewish tailors in Poplar, Stepney and Bethnal Green. It was my task to deliver and collect uniforms from these establishments, which brought me into contact with the so-called 'smatter trade'. Most of the workers sat neatly in line in factory-like establishments or 'sweat shops' from dawn to dusk making good uniforms worth about £20 each. I therefore saw the extensive bomb damage in the East End and observed the destruction of the streets and tenements in Bethnal Green where the tailors lived. Despite these conditions, although looking tired, people seemed unbowed and resolute and maintained their sense of humour. Truly the East Enders were a remarkably loyal breed, tough, and patriotic, even if many of them were communists. I used to listen to their opinions about the conduct of the war: they were particularly well informed about Montgomery's progress once his armies had crossed the Rhine and had moved deep into the Ruhr region.

Back at Mayday Gardens, Alan and I knew that our days in the NFS were numbered even though the V2s were still falling on London. It was officially announced that, as from 1 February, part-time NFS personnel were to be disbanded and that of course included us. We were to be allowed to keep our dark-blue uniforms and heavy overcoats, which were a welcome addition to our winter clothing. We were delighted to be invited to the stand down concert at the Albert Hall where we sat high in the Gods, in a reasonably good position, to see and hear the array of artists who had volunteered to entertain us all. This magnificent occasion was attended by thousands of part-time firemen and support staff and we were impressed by the number of women who had also served with the NFS during the war. To this day we both regret not keeping the stand down concert programme which included so many well-known entertainers such as Tommy Handley, Tessie O'Shea and Tommy Trinder. What a thrill it was for us to be invited to such a concert, particularly as our time in the NFS hadn't always been such a joyous experience, even on a part-time basis, as it had been full of anguish and horror.

Alan and I thought the stand down was a little bit premature since the V2s were still coming in. In fact, just a week before we were formally apprenticed at Waterman's Hall in the City of London, where we pledged to serve our master Alfred Williams, nearby Smithfield Market was devastated by a V2. It hit crowds of shoppers flocking to the meat market and 115 lives were lost with many more injured.

As Alan and I travelled home on the tram after our indenture, we speculated about how really useful we had proved to be to the war effort. We both agreed that we had never carried a single message for the NFS so the idea that we were 'messengers' was a total misnomer. We were, however, useful in other roles; controlling people and traffic and, on other occasions, carrying out actual rescue work. We had been agile and willing rescuers in situations where the rescue involved getting into small cavities to discover casualties and even bringing them to the surface. On one occasion Alan was lowered by rope into the debris to find a way through the rubble to reach into the depths of a wrecked building, which he achieved without too much difficulty although with some personal risk. Both of us were actually quite fearless in such situations and mercifully these acts of reckless disregard for our own lives were but isolated acts of courage not uncommon among the citizens of London. But all of that was now in the past. Freed from the sense of duty we concentrated on becoming lightermen; we were working on diesel-driven tugs as cabin boys and learning the trade from the bottom up. I was on the tug *Rio* and Alan was on the tug *Banco,* both of which were well maintained and skilfully navigated by experienced crews.

Both crews, however, came near to death when a V2 hit our permanent berth at Folly House Wharf, on the Isle of Dogs. We worked a twenty-four-hour watch and the tugs were tied up alongside each other for the night at the Wharf when the missile struck. As it was low water miraculously both tugs were unaffected, despite the destruction of the wharf and the jetty. The concussive blast generated by the explosion had passed overhead leaving both us and our respective tugs intact. We had enjoyed a divine deliverance. How on earth we survived such a huge explosion just thirty or so yards from where we were, standing on the decks, we did not know. I shouted to Alan, 'That rocket is possibly the last of the war.' 'This is how the next war will begin,' he quickly retorted.

The days that followed were memorable, even if events seemed to drag as we waited for news on the defeat of Germany. To begin with, for the first time in our lives, we were earning a living and getting to grips with the idea of our long seven-year apprenticeship. Even at the time I thought this was far too long and couldn't imagine finishing the never-ending process until my early twenties.

Our early days were spent cleaning cabins, handing out ropes, and putting fenders between the tugs and the ships or barges to prevent damage to the tug when we went alongside. The tug skipper required skill and patience when picking up perhaps as many as six barges to tow in line. Each of these was manned by lightermen, who would also finally dock the barge or tie up to a jetty. Not that easy. We were also astonished to see lightermen 'driving' a barge with a long pole and with an outstretched overcoat acting like a sail in order to navigate using the kinetic energy of the wind and the more skilful of them could even drive the barge against the tide. I rather took the view that this job was not for me and that I would prefer to work on the tugs and perhaps become a skipper of a vessel in the fullness of time, say in ten years or so. That seemed to me like an eternity. Perhaps now I was slowly realising that school might have been a better alternative than life on the River Thames yet was it now too late. For the first time in our lives we realised that we needed to repair our lack of formal education. To begin with we would apply ourselves to our trade and learn how best to navigate upstream beneath the bridges that spanned the River Thames and downstream to Gravesend and around to the River Medway. The bridges were the points where the tugs faced their greatest challenge in terms of the skill and knowledge required to judge the depth of the water, the width between the arches of the bridges, and their height in relation to the superstructure of the vessels. We soon also got to know the other special navigation requirements for places like Barking Creek and similar tributaries all the way down the Thames to Benfleet Creek. We loved the vocabulary and the place-names, all of which we were expected to commit to memory as we would be tested on these after the completion of at least two years work. We learnt a little bit about the Upper Pool and Lower Pool, as well as the busy Limehouse Reach, the West India Pier, and the Greenland Dock Entrance. Above all, the romance of Greenwich Reach, which included the splendid Royal Naval College and Greenwich Pier where our great grandfather had been Pier Master and a Master Mariner, captivated us. From the deck of our tugs, moving close to the waterline, we got a unique and unrivalled view of the quays, wharves, and buildings lining both banks of the Thames. The water flowed quickly on both the ebb and incoming tides but proved remarkably lake-like at high water upstream from Galleon's Reach. We both vividly recall passing beneath the historic bridges such as London Bridge or, slightly lower down the river, Tower Bridge, which was often raised to allow the bigger ships access to the upper reaches of the river. My favourite trip was down to Thames Haven where we both often engaged in the quite dangerous work of helping to unload sunken vessels, which had suffered damage through air attacks. Little did we know, and still less were we told, about the wreck which we, with others, were periodically attending in a bid to unload its deadly cargo. This was the wreck of the *Richard Montgomery*, which on 20 August 1944 had run aground and became stuck fast in the sand banks. It was unloaded largely by stevedores from Rochester but finally the ship was abandoned on 25 September 1944 with its remaining cargo amounting to some 3,200 tons of explosives. The real problem, in common with all the Liberty ships built in weeks or months rather than in years, was that they were prone to break up in bad weather conditions. This particular ship carried a large consignment of shells stored in the hold with the detonators stacked on the deck exposed to the elements. She was berthed off the north edge of Sheerness Middle Sand, off the coast of the Isle of Sheppey, where she still remains to this day.

My tug, the *Rio,* would be sent by Union Lighterage to tow away the barges loaded with high explosives from the ship so when we went alongside we were obliged to extinguish our cooking stove and the 'hands' were prohibited from smoking. The danger was palpable and the hapless citizens of Sheerness lived in peril, and still do, from a dangerous cargo, which, if ignited, would hurl a column of mud, metal, and munitions almost 10,000 feet into the air. Such an explosion would cause widespread damage to Sheerness with the risk of considerable loss of life, but of this we knew nothing as we worked alongside the wreck in the Thames Estuary.

Enemy action had resulted in the sinking of ships both big and small as they navigated their way to the Port of London but, mercifully, most of our experience was related to the towing of the barges into and out of the docks. We were exhausted by twenty-four hours of pretty continuous work, even though we enjoyed the forty-eight hours off watch. Our fellow crew members, the skipper, the second mate, and the two engineers, were, however, mindful of our age and we often got more sleep than they did when encouraged to 'get our heads down' in the small but comfortable stern cabin. Mr Smith my skipper (I never did know his first name and we wouldn't have been allowed to use it anyway) had access to the more capacious cabin, in the forward part of the vessel, which I was expected to scrub clean as well as polishing the brasswork surrounding the fog bell just below the wheelhouse. Personally I was not very happy with the arduous nature of the work involved in the apprenticeship and began to get restive; Alan less so. In order to alleviate my situation I concentrated on getting back into uniform by rejoining the Army Cadets where, by getting war certificate 'A' parts one and two, I gained rapid promotion. Ashore most of our friends, including our girlfriends, led more settled and apparently more satisfactory lives as the war entered its terminal phase. The news that British forces had crossed the Rhine and were preparing for the final battle on the Western Front coincided with a specially cooked lunch at home on Easter Monday, 2 April 1945, to celebrate Germany's impending defeat. Dad remarked, uncharacteristically, 'This is it at last.' Alfred Williams was right and within days the US 9th Army, which we had come across in Somerset during our ATC camp, had reached the Elbe. Then, with Berlin on the point of collapse, we learnt from the BBC that President Roosevelt was dead. He died from a cerebral haemorrhage on 12 April 1945. Alan said that Roosevelt's visit to Russia had killed him off and that Stalin's refusal to leave his country to meet Roosevelt at a more convenient place was a terrible mistake. How could Stalin expect a sick man to go to Russia? The sad news of his death was offset by the thought of victory and the thought of peace as the Russians and the Americans linked up with the British forces and took Hamburg and the suburbs of Bremen. We sensed the historic magnitude of these events just as we had sensed the magnitude of the fall of France in 1940. We all asked the same question – when will Victory be declared? As we reported to work on the tugs on 7 May we awaited events with growing impatience.

13

The End Game

Alan and I were both on the River Thames when the Second World War came to an end on Monday 7 May 1945 at 02.41 Greenwich Mean Time, as my tug, the *Rio*, made its way up the river towards Tower Bridge with six barges in tow. The rumours and counter rumours of the previous day had confused everyone but we were convinced that the king would speak to the nation that day. The tug did not possess a radio or any other direct means of communication, which made me feel strangely isolated on the river, despite being in the middle of London. Alan, on board the *Banco*, experienced the same sense of being cut off and like me, he felt we should be part of a victorious, deliriously happy nation. Strangely the end of the war did not excite either of us very much; there was none of the frisson we experienced when war was declared. The truth was that victory now seemed inevitable and something of an anticlimax in part because the government appeared reluctant to tell the people that victory could now be declared.

We constantly asked: 'When will VE Day be officially announced?' We had noticed, a few days earlier, that the BBC news was read without giving the name of the announcer as it had been prior to the start of the war. For us this heralded the end of the war if voices such as those of Wilfred Pickles, with his pleasant Yorkshire accent, were no longer deemed to be the voice of the BBC. Alan had clear, if dogmatic, ideas

about what the end of the war really meant and he now
switched his interest to the home front. He spoke to me
about the need for the nation to be rewarded with plenty
of jobs, adequate wages, and pensions. He wanted to see
greater provision of security for ordinary people. We largely
agreed on these matters but our views counted for nothing
– we hadn't even got the vote. My interest still centred on
the war and its wider strategic consequences. I was now
thinking about what would happen in Europe, to Germany in
particular, once the war finished, which, as I reminded Alan,
still left the unresolved problem of how best to defeat the
Japanese whose fanaticism was clear for all to see. This war
was not over yet and it could drag on against the Japanese
for years. 'On this day of all days you might have been a bit
more elated!' Alan said.

The war against Japan could perhaps last for another
two years or so, yet the pressure to break up the coalition
government under Winston Churchill had now become
inevitable and Labour decided to press for an early general
election, the first since 1935.

The day before the formal end of the war in Europe we
were on our respective tugs punching up the river with just
twelve hours of our watch left. As we slowly navigated
upstream the merchant ships moored along the banks of
the Thames were building up steam so that their sirens could
mark the end of the war. Some were already marking the
victory loudly and soon other ships joined in. Their excited
crews knew more than we did, isolated as we were on board
our little tugs; Germany had surrendered and Hitler was
dead. His body had been burnt on 2 May as the survivors of
the Berlin garrison surrendered. On 7 May 1945 hostilities
ceased; the war was over yet the peace was not yet official.

On the Thames the cacophony of the ship sirens was now
at full blast as the *Rio* pumped upstream. Mr Smith, our

taciturn skipper, shouted from his wheelhouse that once we got the barges to Fulham Barge Roads, we would return to Folly House Wharf on the Isle of Dogs to tie up for the night and then we would be then free to go home. This was the only time I had heard him say anything at all. I saw Alan standing on his tug the *Banco*, which was ahead of us upstream, waving his arms in a spontaneous outburst of joy. Some twenty minutes later our tugs passed under London Bridge and then Tower Bridge where crowds had gathered in an excitable state. Fires were being lit in the East End of London, which cast a flickering glow strangely reminiscent of the Blitz of 1940. We left the tugs in silence in the early hours wrapped in own private thoughts as we cycled home.

The streets were deserted at 4 a.m. Alan and I both agreed that we would cycle home rather than stay on board for the night or for what was left of it. It was now starting to get light as we entered the Greenwich foot tunnel without seeing a living soul, and the south side of the Thames at Greenwich was also deserted. Had the people there not heard the splendid news? While the East Enders were deliriously happy and dancing round open fires, the people living around Greenwich Park and Blackheath were apparently sleeping. We cycled through the park beneath the Royal Observatory seeing only a fox but peace was not just a cliché because, as dawn broke, it was greeted by a chorus of birds who had seemed to sing in celebration.

We quickly crossed Blackheath towards Kidbrooke and Mayday Gardens. We noticed that the entire road was still blacked out. Not a single light was on. This at first seemed astonishing yet perhaps not. Our neighbours had taken to their beds to enjoy an unbroken night's sleep without having to wonder whether the air-raid siren would sound off its menacing warning. We knocked on our front door as we were not allowed to have keys of our own; a privilege that only came once we reached the age of twenty-one. Suddenly the light in the front bedroom came on. Dad came downstairs slowly in his pyjamas with Mum standing behind him peering down anxiously from the top of the stairs as he unlocked the door. 'We weren't expecting you until tomorrow,' he said, making no reference to the end of the war or any attempt to offer warm greetings to his sons standing on the doorstep. We entered the house and Mum simply warned us that the water was now too cold for a bath so we should undress, go straight to bed and not create a noise. Our attempts to sleep ended fairly quickly as the worst storm since the outbreak of the war bought a violent thunder and forked lightning igniting Mayday Gardens' barrage balloon, which had done its best to protect us for over six years. Alan whispered to me that he distinctly remembered that the outbreak of war on 3 September 1939 had been greeted with a similar storm; we both agreed that this was an eerie coincidence.

The next day, though short of sleep, we caught the train to Charing Cross station in London to join the crowds gathering along The Strand to celebrate victory over Germany. Now the fun would begin. We were swept along by a tidal wave of humanity as we neared Buckingham Palace at the end of the Mall, where we hoped to see the Royal Princesses, Elizabeth and Margaret. Indeed, ten years later I was to dance with Princess Margaret at a commemoration ball at Keele University. The appearance of the Royal Family on the balcony of Buckingham Palace embodied not only our sense of pride, but perhaps a sense of relief and disappointment as well, as the Royal Family came out onto the balcony of the Palace with an apparent lack of enthusiasm. Perhaps they were simply tired of the their repeated appearances to acknowledge the cheering crowds so, after about an hour of jostling and shouting, we decided to go home to Mayday

Gardens where, after a good night's sleep, we attended our own victory celebration organised by our parents and neighbours with a modest supply of cakes and sandwiches. Clearly much preparation had gone into this well-conceived street party.

Our own excitement rose when we noticed, in the half-light of evening, that the beautiful daughter of a local teacher had appeared with her father. She was a young girl of seventeen, whom Alan and I had greatly admired at a distance. Her somewhat alcoholic father, who was a communist, remarked to me, 'It's the Soviets that won the war, not Churchill.' I replied to the effect that VE day belonged to the British people. A general election would soon be held, which might sweep from power the Conservative-dominated coalition government. This prediction appeared to please him but I was, in fact, by no means certain that breaking up the coalition government was a sensible thing to do before the defeat of Japan.

Yet on that summer's evening, the small boy of barely ten who had had to leave his home to escape the bombing some six year previously, was now home for good and lying in the tall grass kissing the teacher's pretty daughter! Dad was only a few yards away talking to Mum and Alan was looking for me! Had my mother seen me she would have been deeply shocked to see her elder son, lying with a girl alongside the NFS water tank. Audrey had long dark hair, beautiful green eyes and slim limbs. In a close embrace this highly developed seventeen-year-old told me that sex was for pleasure and should be enjoyed at least twice a day. I should banish my guilt. She, like her father, was a Marxist and so she had a dialectical explanation for everything. Sex, she told me, was not just for procreation but also for recreation. How progressive she seemed! She then indicated she was prepared to go further if 'I wanted to' – although I didn't really know how. 'I'll show you how,' she said but afterwards apologised for sexually manipulating me although I certainly didn't mind. A few weeks later Alan told me that he had also met Audrey in the woods and she had likewise expertly defused his passion. I could not resist telling my brother that she had done a similar thing to me. Sex was fun and we boys wanted more of it.

As the war drew to its close we discussed the evidence, which was uncovered when the British Army liberated the Belsen concentration camp, that Jewish people were maltreated and murdered as a deliberate act of policy. Despite repeated denials by ordinary Germans that such things ever occurred, or if they did, they were ignorant of such brutality, the callous and systematic elimination of the Jews and others was now clear for all to see. The BBC carried awful accounts of the conditions in Belsen and the related efforts by the British to provide food and medical care for the woeful inmates.

Yet Dad initially refused to believe these reports, which he dismissed as propaganda rather like that said by the Allies in the First World War. Mum, Alan and I all agreed that Dad on this occasion was simply wrong. The Germans had set to intimidate and exterminate the Jewish race. Over time Dad accepted what was being said, which merely accorded with the increasing number of reliable reports now available to the press and radio as the inhuman behaviour of the German troops became common knowledge. How much the ordinary Germans knew or approved of this behaviour was endlessly debated.

This debate sparked the biggest rift with Dad of the entire war. We accused him of being anti-Jewish as were many working men of his generation working in the docklands area of the East End of London. Dad defended his position with vigour by saying that the Jews were over-concentrated in areas such as retail and BBC radio. In his experience the Jews never seemed to be open to influence beyond their own tightly knit families and communities. Alan said that this argument was exaggerated especially by the Black Shirts, who had ritually exploited anti-Jewish feelings in the East End.

This heated and pugnacious discussion opened up a rift with Dad, which took months to heal. Unfortunately his views were quite widely shared by others who, like him, were otherwise moderate Labour voters and trade unionists. We knew that Dad had virtually no personal contact with Jews so we resolved to have Jewish friends. Dad accepted this and his prejudicial attitude gradually gave way to a more reasoned approach. Killing Jews because they were Jews was wrong and evil and, although we were too adolescent to know it, we had in effect defined genocide – a crime which was later declared to be contrary to international law.

We were much vexed by this row with our father, which was the first instance of us standing up to him on a question that transcended the usual domestic disputes. Even our Aunt Ada, when she heard of this dispute, attributed his vehemence to his frequent bad temper rather than a deeply held prejudice towards the Jews towards whom she herself was in fact rather less than sympathetic anyway. She repeated the widely accepted view that East End Jews were the first to flee from the Blitz and the first to colonise the platforms of the London Underground by monopolising this safe haven for themselves.

Eventually we mentioned all of this to our close friend John Bray who said that he had heard similar remarks made by his relations and his father in particular. Yet we three boys remained puzzled by the anti-Semitic feelings, especially in the light of the shocking events revealed on the BBC about Belsen and elsewhere. We concluded that the Jews must have done something so heinous to arouse such wroth.

Alan and I then turned to Gwen, who was now living at home prior to going up to Oxford, for an opinion about the issue of anti-Semitism. She said that for 2,000 years Christians had blamed the Jews for the death of Christ and, although there were other reasons for Hitler's anti-Semitism, the truth was that the extreme historical Christian obsession with the death of Christ, particularly in Luther's Germany, eventually led to the concentration camps on a massive industrial scale. How right she was. 'Were there any innocent Germans?' we asked. 'Probably not,' she replied.

As spring moved into summer, with the very real prospect of a protracted war against Japan, we heard the dramatic news on the BBC that Hiroshima had been destroyed on 6 August and Nagasaki had been eviscerated on the 9th, and in both cases by atomic bombs. Japan was now defeated and so was belatedly prepared to accept unconditional surrender with the proviso that the Emperor be allowed to continue as head of state. The Allies swiftly agreed to this: the Second World War was over.

14

Politics Not War

Both of us by now had decided one way or another to enter politics; Alan joined the Greenwich Labour Party and, later, I decided to join the Young Conservatives in the City of London and went to their lunchtime meetings while working in Union Lighterage Company's City offices as part of my apprenticeship. Alan joined the Labour League of Youth out of a growing sense of conviction, while I joined the Young Conservatives with no conviction except that this offered the possibility of meeting pretty girls who were looking for eligible husbands working in City banks.

Alan and I now readied ourselves for the post-war world. We both accepted that the status quo could not be maintained, nor that it should be. Alan asked me to find out from my newly acquired Tory friends whether Mr Churchill had a proper mandate to offer the electorate. I asked Alan to define what he thought a mandate was. He said it included a series of commitments to enable the voter to decide whether to vote for the proposals in the manifesto. In 1945, the Conservatives had a less detailed manifesto than Mr Atlee's Labour Party and, although I didn't really know then about the importance of a manifesto, I subsequently found that the explanation lay in the differing attitudes to Parliamentary politics. Conservative MPs were considered to be representatives who had the right to choose to speak, and vote, according to their conscience and not merely to adhere to what the party demanded. Labour Members of Parliament, however, were expected to stick to the party's manifesto and to regard themselves as mandated to speak according to the party's line, thus regarding themselves as delegates. I soon reasoned that it was probably not quite like that; once in Parliament MPs of both parties could choose to defy the Party Whips and speak more freely if they chose so to do. Later, when Alan was elected to the House of Commons, he did modify his view and saw the merit in giving MPs some discretion and freedom to vote on matters of conscience.

Alan possessed an intuitive grasp of the political process and we discussed whether or not the wartime coalition government should come to an end with our friends? Alan thought that normal politics should be resumed immediately. I took the view that the wartime coalition, one of the most successful governments of modern times, should continue until most of the troops were demobilised which would allow time for a more considered view about the future for Britain in the post-war era.

We now also had time to reflect on our personal contributions, if any, to the outcome of the war. To begin with could we, as children, really have played a meaningful part in the worst war in history? We sat beneath the castle in Castle Woods, John, Barry, Alan, and I, and decided to adopt a formal procedure with Alan presenting the case that we, and by extension, other children, did actually contribute to Britain's victory and that we had made a real difference. Alan argued that right from the start of the war we had tried to join in. This ambition remained firm and persistent in the face of the difficulties mostly raised by our parents and teachers. Alan said that they did not understand us because as adults they saw things differently. They hoped that the war would be a short one while we had hoped it would be a long one so that we could be in it when we grew up: they proved to be wrong and we were right!

Alan's view was that this war, regardless of how it was fought, slowly became a total war in which civilians were as important as the fighting men. He did not think that the initial German Blitzkrieg attacks could have, alone, resulted in a German victory because, in the event, Britain had won the Battle of Britain in 1940 and therefore our island became the platform on which the grand alliance could be built and from which Europe could be liberated. Alan also said that the Soviet Union's heroic resistance in the face of the Nazi onslaught made victory possible but that it did not, by itself, achieve this.

Our own personal part in these events might appear slight but we twins never wavered in our support for the war and therefore perhaps we played a small part in keeping other children around us positive and resolute. Between the Blitz in 1940 to the V1 and V2 attacks in 1944, we changed from being boy spectators to real civil defence participants in the war effort. Other children were equally involved, either as victims of the war or as belligerents in the final stages of the war, while in Germany Hitler's boy soldiers actually fought the Russians in Berlin. If this was a people's war then only the old or the very young were less than crucial. We had tried to contribute to the home front right from the start. Alan said that the history of the Second World War would be incomplete unless the part played by the Army Cadets, the Air Cadets, and the NFS Messengers, not forgetting the Home Guard, was recognised. We were the next generation who had been forced to grow up before their time and, in so doing, had become more than mere spectators.

It was a great pity that only John, Barry, and I were privileged enough to hear this diatribe, which was curiously impressive and persuasive if less than well thought through. Alan the politician quickly got to his point: 'The state must be forced to share the nation's wealth more equally by rewarding the ordinary people who made victory possible. The nation at large, including the children who had helped, had won the war and the welfare state should be their reward.' His dogmatic approach impressed John but Barry was less sure that ordinary people would be rewarded given the nature of capitalism.

I then tried to argue the opposite but without much passion and gave a rather less heroic explanation of our conduct since, against my better judgement, I wanted to believe everything Alan had said. I said that perhaps we had rationalised our failure at school with escapist day-dreaming of the worst kind and that, even more disturbingly, we had failed to see this at the time. Alan was rather more messianic and idealistic and had, in fact, been the prime mover behind the homework strikes which got us expelled. He had developed a pathological dislike of the academically gifted, especially if they attempted to patronise him. This made him a first-class rebel, but one who was also daring and not afraid to speak bluntly if it served his interests. He was frequently the initiator of everything we did to get into the war. He was always ready, like Churchill, to go over the top in some desperate manoeuvre. His self-confidence was infectious.

At school, in the Cadets, and in the fire service, Alan excelled in getting us noticed. Everyone knew us as 'The Twins' with Alan in the lead even if his follies were jointly shared. My advantage lay elsewhere; I was better at conforming which explains why, in the Army Cadets, I rose to the dizzy rank of full Sergeant whereas Alan never rose above the rank of Corporal; a rank he achieved by a remarkable act of self-promotion when he managed to trick our commanding officer. Alan sent a telegram to himself saying, 'Full corporal stripes up by Wednesday,' and signed it Captain Levy, so when Alan duly turned up at cadets wearing his new stripes, Captain Levy immediately challenged him. Alan then produced the telegram which Captain Levy dismissed as just a cruel joke, but he would allow Alan to keep the rank in order to embarrass the perpetrator of this nasty trick! This revealed Alan at his ingenious best.

I took a different view over our schooling, wondering why we couldn't have attended school and acquired knowledge as well as trying to involve ourselves in the war. Most normal children took that route, no doubt to their eventual advantage. Surely this is what we should have done? Instead we chose to sacrifice our future in order to satisfy our egos. We exploited every opportunity to avoid going to school or to take our lessons seriously when we were there. It can't have been easy for our teachers, many of whom had been either expecting to retire soon or who had actually retired but were patriotic enough to return to the overcrowded wartime classrooms in order to contribute to the war effort. My Dad also spent a considerable amount of money on our education, at some personal cost, with the not unreasonable expectation that we would rise to the occasion and 'pull our socks up', as he would say, and benefit from a good opportunity as had our elder sister, hence my father's reference to us as 'The Duffers'.

By 1945 I felt that we had definitely made the wrong choice, but that all was not lost and that we could retrieve the situation. And eventually we did. Sylvia Holt, John Bray's girlfriend and future wife and Alan's muse, who was still at the Eltham High School, received a message, via her headmistress, from King George VI, which appeared to confirm our view that the 'war' children had contributed in various ways to Britain's victory. This message was sent to all children still at school on 8 June 1946, just over a year after VE Day.

Today, we celebrate victory. I send this personal message to you and all other boys and girls at school, for you have shared in the hardships and dangers of a total war and you have shared no less in the triumph of the Allied Nations.

I know you will always feel proud to belong to a county which was capable of such supreme effort; proud, too, of parents and elder brothers and sisters, who by their courage, endurance and enterprise, brought victory. May these qualities be yours as you grow up and join in the common effort to establish among the nations of the world unity and peace. George R.I
King George VI

We felt vindicated and rejoiced in the British success. In 1945 the Ministry of Information published a book entitled *What Britain Has Done,* and rightly said that until the whole story could be told it would be a grave disservice, not only to Britain, but also to her allies in the common cause, if an excessive reticence were to prevent a general understanding of what Britain had done in the Second World War. We felt that we too could claim a part in the war effort, however small.

Geoffrey Lee Williams,
1946.

Yet what was it about Britain that we loved so much and which we also identified in our neighbours? Well it was George Orwell who had noticed a 'privateness' about English life, a love of personal liberty and a hatred of intrusion by authority. That was the basis of our intense patriotism. Britain was essentially, if only briefly, a united nation. A new age was emerging out of the cauldron of war – the social democratic age. However, this new age would not arise quickly since post-war reconstruction would take time.

Actually for us the war had only ended in a formal sense in 1945, because its deprivations actually escalated during the dreadful winter of 1946/47, when thick snow fell and the entire country was gripped by arctic temperatures. The age of austerity continued as food supplies diminished, heralding an even more draconian rationing system than that experienced during the war years, during which domestic electricity was cut off for five hours each day to conserve coal supplies. It was proving to be a bitter peace.

But with the onset of the summer of 1947, which proved to be a hot one in all respects, we rejoined the Army Cadets and were soon promoted to senior ranks, as by now we both possessed War Certificate A and B, the first written tests we had ever passed. Dressed in better uniforms and with new equipment we looked the part as we were now taller and so the uniforms fitted us well. Alan still enjoyed being an apprentice Waterman and Lighterman but I merely endured it, particularly the hours that we were expected to work. I wanted a more conventional lifestyle. It appeared obvious to us that Britain was in steep decline as a world super power so we hoped that the brilliant summer of 1947 was the promise of better things to come. We followed external events with our usual pertinacity. The Marshall Plan had kick-started the Western European recovery and Alan was by now strongly committed to the Labour Party which, in the summer of 1945, had enjoyed a landslide victory. The new government promised radical change along the lines that Alan had been talking about ever since the middle part of the war. This included widespread nationalisation, including the introduction of the National Health Service, as well as state control of coal mining, electricity and supply, and the railways. Military expenditure, which was far higher than before the war, now included a research and development programme leading to the deployment of Britain's own atomic bomb. We all recognised the reality of Britain's situation which, in the short term, led to savage cuts in public spending at home culminating in the humiliating devaluation of sterling, meaning the nation had had to become a supplicant of the United States which, in the event, proved to be much to Britain's advantage as the Cold War with the Soviet Union had set in with a vengeance.

The post-war settlement and Britain's survival now depended upon the recovery of Western Europe and with it heightened access to the immense resources of the Western Hemisphere. Alan and I agreed that a great power conflict was about to unfold, which would have immense implications for our generation and which could be comparable to the experience of total war. We felt that we were part of that younger generation that had yet to reap the rewards of victory, but that they would come. Just as the war against Germany had been a long slog so the post-war recovery would come in due course. We were determined to be patient and indeed, by the mid-1950s, a remarkable change in Britain's relative prosperity had occurred. During the next twenty years Alan would become a Member of Parliament and my long career as a university academic was underway.

As twin boys we liked to agree on most things, if we could, and we both passionately believed that the Second World

War was a *necessary* war not just an *accidental* occurrence. It was, we had thought, about the survival of Mayday Gardens – a metaphor for the greater national interest.

Under the hot sun of that glorious summer of 1947 all of us, Alan, John, Barry, and I, gathered in the shade of the so-called aeroplane tree in nearby Little Woods. This tree had the outline shape of a bomber and it was on its stout branches that we had enacted our aerial combats as children. We were now struggling to identify what was the national interest in the aftermath of the war. For over a thousand years it had been the need to see off all foreign invaders and the concomitant occupation of the country. Hitler and the Nazis were the right enemy and the policy of inflicting a crippling and total defeat on Germany was certainly the right objective. Were we now about to face a similar, or worse, threat from Stalin's Russia? The 'Cold War' had started, although Alan and I disagreed somewhat about how best to conduct this ideological war without provoking a real one. The Cold War, however, persisted for another forty years bringing in its wake the strategic nuclear deadlock upon which the peace of the world rested. We strongly approved of NATO, about which we were later to write several books; we believed in the Anglo-American alliance as a force for good. Stalin's Russia was a bad model to follow: it was a terrible accident of history.

During the immediate post-war period we felt the need to try and assess who we were and where we stood as we entered our mid- and late teens. We were now part of the country's workforce and all our immediate friends had jobs. We were therefore, to all intents and purposes, young adults but with this difference – we had never really enjoyed a normal boyhood, whatever that was. We had much to make up for and so, in the process of growing up, we went through a painful transition to adjust to the realities of being mature.

Alan's political consciousness was almost displaced by the sight of girls in their pretty summer dresses and, while I liked Handel's aria 'Endless Pleasure' from his opera *Semele*, Alan preferred the more sentimental songs of the day such as Jo Stafford's 'Long Ago and Far Away' or Doris Day's 'Bewitched, Bothered and Bewildered'. We both enjoyed Joe Loss's 'In the Mood' and most of all Geraldo's 'That Lovely Weekend'.

At the end of the 1940s we were both conscripted as national servicemen in the RAF for two years. I was later commissioned in the Territorial Army in 1960, while Alan served as a special constable with the Metropolitan Police.

What did we miss about the war? We certainly missed the excitement and the danger, and even the noise of war – the falling bombs, the Ack-Ack guns opening up, the hideous roar of the Doodlebugs, and the extraordinary sound caused by the arrival of a V2 missile. We even missed the wailing of the air-raid siren and the comforting sight of the barrage balloons, as well as the whole ethos of working together for a common end – the defeat of the Nazis. In the fullness of time and in a totally different strategic environment, we rejoiced in the final death throes of the Cold War and the collapse of the Soviet Union, which we regarded as yet another manifestation of the unacceptable governance by totalitarian rule. We were, to quote Lord William Rees-Mogg, 'part of the Spitfire generation', which had a hard-nosed attitude towards those who threatened our liberties. Thus we never saw ourselves as non-belligerents.

The brutal truth was that in total war no-one is entirely unengaged or neutral. Innocent civilians rarely existed either in Britain or in Germany. They were inevitable participants in the war effort and so, perhaps, became inevitably legitimate targets when the bombing and destruction of German cities perforce became the Allied commanders' strategy. We boys, in our crude and simplistic reasoning, shared this view and therefore we submerged our identities in a seamless struggle to be on the winning, and the right, side.

22 Mayday Gardens, *c.* 1990.

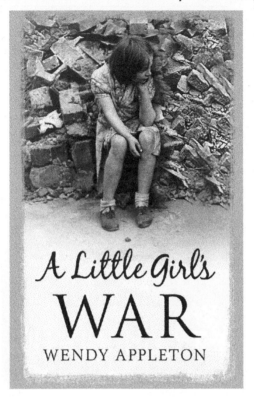

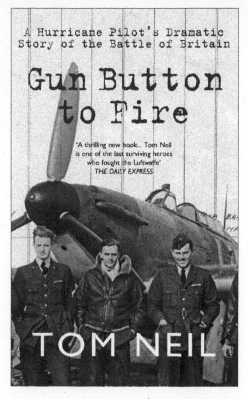